WELLSPRINGS OF LIFE

UNDERSTANDING PROVERBS

"Understanding is a wellspring of life
unto him that hath it . . ."
(Proverbs 16:22)

By Donald Orthner
Using the King James Version of Scripture

ISBN 0-9622942-0-9 KJV

Published by Adon Books
7 Donington Dr.
Greenville, SC 29615

Printed in the USA
First printing: March 1989
Second printing: June 1989
Third printing: September 1992

Credits:
Cover and illustrations by Del Thompson, Greenville, SC.
Color separation by For Color, Inc., Milwaukee, WI.

Dedicated to

David, Carol, and Dale,

whose wholehearted interest and involvement
in launching this project
made it all worthwhile

About the Author

In preparing *Wellsprings of Life,* Don Orthner combined extensive experience in business analysis and in management presentations with a deep love for God's Word. The result is this penetrating, application-oriented presentation of Proverbs' timeless truths.

The author's love for God's Word was nurtured from childhood by godly parents and grandparents who faithfully served their Lord in the pastorate, foreign missions, and local churches. The Lord had a different avenue of service, however, for Don: using his business abilities in support of many different Christian ministries.

A native of Michigan, Don earned his Bachelor's and Master's degrees in business administration at the University of Michigan, majoring in finance and economics. For the next 25 years, he worked at Ford Motor Company's world headquarters in international and corporate financial management. He found time, however, to serve on the boards of directors of several Christian ministries and as an active lay worker in a large Bible-preaching church. Don presently provides business and financial consulting services to Christian ministries and Christian-owned businesses in Greenville, South Carolina.

Foreword

The blessed man of Psalm 1 is deeply rooted by rivers of water. I've always experienced a refreshing when contemplating this striking visual that God uses to portray the man who meditates in His Word both day and night. It is no coincidence that Scripture frequently parallels the blessedness of life in the Word and the refreshment of life by rivers of water.

The flesh of both man and beast is about two-thirds water (blood serum is a full 92 percent water!). Every bodily process requires it, and without it, life is impossible. I was overwhelmed with the reality of this recently while flying over the burnt, red sands of Australia's forsaken outback. From 30,000 feet, the barren surface below looked like something angrily scoured over with a rusty Brillo pad. The appalling problem is the utter absence of moisture. Horizon to horizon, the jagged cliffs rise like bared fangs over miles of bone-dry chasms in the earth's fiery surface. And though I strained my eyes for it, there wasn't the faintest sign of anything green—or even withered yellow.

Nothing lives without water. No wonder, then, that the Word, so essential for every sprig of spiritual life, is paralleled to water. Both are indispensable—not just for portions of life, but for **all** of it!

It would be inappropriate to call one part of God's Word more indispensable than another. But if there is any book of it that seems to water the greatest variety of spiritual needs, it would have to be Proverbs. The topics treated in its short, pithy sayings are almost endless. No dimension of life on earth is omitted from its discussions. Like a well yielding water for every new growth of life, Proverbs pours out wisdom for every aspect of spiritual living.

The book you hold in your hands, *Wellsprings of Life,* is one of the most valuable tools for drawing from Proverbs' well that I've ever used. When Don Orthner first showed me a rough draft of this project some five years ago, I felt certain that it would be welcomed by laymen and pastors alike. Although there are several good commentaries on Proverbs available today, there is not, to my knowledge, another work so extensive in its topical treatment of the book.

Proverbs was meant to be studied topically. But unfortunately, topical study involves a lavish expenditure of time collating hundreds of texts whose thematic correspondence may not be readily apparent to the casual reader. It also requires a gift for systematizing larger subjects into more manageable subsets. Many of us could type out a list of verses on a single subject, such as, "the use of our tongue." But to be able to **classify** that teaching is beyond many students of the Bible. *Wellsprings of Life* includes that special touch of systematizing that lays bare the immediate application of these studies to life.

Those of us who love and study Proverbs will probably find ourselves turning first to this book the next time we launch a topical study of Solomon's sayings. (Any preacher glancing through the way these topics are outlined will find himself tempted just to preach them almost verbatim!) I'm grateful to Don and his family for the hundreds of hours that went into making this study available to others. Like them, I trust that the Lord will richly bless the use of this fine volume in enabling believers to draw deeply from Proverbs' well.

Mark Minnick
Professor of Bible
Bob Jones University

Preface

Proverbs is unique in Scripture in that its very structure invites us to study the book topically. It introduces and then revisits a great many important subjects in a seemingly random order. Thus a reader who wants to find and correlate all the teaching on any one subject faces a real challenge.

Wellsprings of Life is designed to increase the blessing and lessen the task of studying Proverbs topically. This book collects all of the verses on a single subject, so that the reader can examine them as a unit. The insight provided by the verses' combined message often far exceeds the understanding gleaned from isolated verses.

Wellsprings of Life is primarily a devotional study guide and topical handbook. As such, it will be useful to young people and adults, as well as to families. Sunday school teachers and youth directors also will find it helpful for preparing lessons on Proverbs, and both laymen and clergy can use it in preparing topical devotional talks.

The seed for this book was planted by a Christian speaker who challenged families to work together on projects for their mutual spiritual benefit. By way of example, he exhorted, "Go through the book of Proverbs together and categorize each verse according to its topic." Two years later, while going through Proverbs in family devotions, we decided to take up that challenge.

My original intent was to work with David, Carol, and Dale (aged ten through eight at that time) to compile a handbook in which they could readily find God's answers in Proverbs for the decisions and temptations they would face as they entered their teenage and then college years. Along the way, however, a number of Christian leaders in a variety of ministries encouraged me to prepare the book for publication.

Working with our children on a Ping-Pong table full of cutout verses (over 10 years ago now) made even the logistics of the project enjoyable. Dale's more recent computer skills and his entering all 915 verses of Proverbs into separate files on my PC made it possible to produce the final product; otherwise, the book could still be an unsightly collection of photocopied verses taped on tablet paper under handwritten headings. My dear wife, Ellen, patiently proofread all of the computer verse files. Years of faithful encouragement given by Dr. Robert Teachout, formerly of Detroit Baptist Theological Seminary, and Dr. Mark Minnick, of Bob Jones University, also helped carry the project through to completion.

My prayer is that this book will be of great practical, spiritual value in the lives of many Christians of all ages. As the book indicates, the real message of Proverbs goes well beyond "Obey and be blessed" or "Be skillful and succeed"; it is rather "Be ye holy; for I am holy"—in every area and detail of life! Proverbs, as much as any Scripture, requires that we be doers of the Word and not hearers only.

Donald Orthner

Note

This book generally presents foundational topics first, followed by those that primarily involve application and expansion of foundational principles. Each chapter of *Wellsprings of Life,* however, as well as each major section of each chapter, can be used independently.

Each verse in Proverbs is included in the topical outline at least once, and most are included under two or more topics. Chapters 1-5 and 7-9 of Proverbs have additional value when each chapter is studied in full; these are outlined in the "Introduction" (chapters 1 and 2) and under "The Believer" (chapters 3 and 4), "Wisdom" (chapters 8 and 9), and "Immorality" (chapters 5 and 7).

The King James Version is used throughout. On occasion, when the meaning of that translation may not be clear, an interpretive word or phrase is inserted in brackets, to show that it is added.

Contents

Chapter   **Page**

1   Introduction — Why Proverbs?

   The Purpose and Premise of Proverbs 2
   The Principal Propositions of Proverbs 3
   A Preview of Proverbs 5
   The Power and Profit of Proverbs 7
   The Providers of Proverbs 8

2   The Almighty God — Our Father

   God's Power and Sovereignty 12
   God's Wisdom 13
   God's Delights and Displeasures 15
   God's Actions and Responses 17
   God's Word 21

3   Life or Death — Everyone's Choice

   The Fear of the Lord 26
   True Life 28
   Death 30
   Sowing and Reaping 34

4   The True Believer

   The Believer's Priorities 38
   The Believer's Objectives 40
   The Believer's Life 43
   The Believer's Blessings 45
   The Believer's Protection 47

5   Invaluable Wisdom

   The Nature of Wisdom 50
   The Benefits of Wisdom 53
   Comparisons and Contrasts to Wisdom 56
   The Constant Call of Wisdom 57

6 Knowledge and Instruction —
Building Blocks for Life

    Learning and Knowledge........................62
    Instruction and Counsel 65
    Reproof and Correction 67

7 The Disciplined Heart and Mind

    Thoughts 72
    Pride 74
    Humility 76
    Prudence and Caution 78

8 Temperament and Emotions —
Causes and Effects

    Happiness and Joy 82
    Peace and Satisfaction 85
    Sorrow and Grief 87
    Anger and Hatred............................90

9 Powerful Words and Speech

    Pure and Constructive Speech 94
    Controlled Speech 96
    Truthful Versus Deceitful Speech 98
    Perverse and Harmful Speech 100

10 Godly Character in Action

    Love and Kindness..........................104
    Generosity..................................106
    Faithfulness.................................107
    Peace With Others Versus Strife 110
    Honor and Respect..........................113

11 The Successful Home and Family

    The Home 118
    Men and IIusbands 119
    Women and Wives..........................121
    Parents and Children 124
    Sons and Daughters 127

12   Special Relationships With Others

Friends 130
Neighbors 133
Rulers and Leaders 135
Citizens 138

13   Principles for Work and Business

Work 142
Laziness 144
Business Principles 146
Financial Practices 149

14   Material Possessions — Servant or Master?

The Believer's Possessions 152
Limitations and Dangers of Riches 154
Covetousness and Greed 157
Poverty and the Poor 159
Food and Eating 162

15   Sin and Its Curse

Sin and the Sinner 166
Temptation and Deliverance 169
Strong Drink 171
Immorality Versus Chastity 173
Immorality's Deception and Destruction 176
Shame and Disgrace 179

16   Those Who Do Not Heed God

The Natural Man 184
The Naive and Simple 185
The Fool 187
The Scoffer 192
The Wicked 193

17   Lessons From Nature

Parallels Between Nature and Personal Traits 202
Parallels Between Nature and Daily Living 205
Parallels Between Nature and Injurious People 208
Examples in Nature of Wisdom and Strength 210

18 Summary and Conclusion

The Overall Message of Proverbs 214
Desires and Goals 216
Finding God's Will 220

Subject Index 223

Chapter 1

Introduction — Why Proverbs?

Bow down thine ear, and hear the words of the wise, and apply thine heart unto my knowledge. For it is a pleasant thing if thou keep them within thee; they shall withal be fitted in thy lips. That thy trust may be in the Lord, I have made known to thee this day, even to thee. Have not I written to thee excellent things in counsels and knowledge, that I might make thee know the certainty of the words of truth, that thou mightest answer the words of truth to them that send unto thee?

(22:17-21)

Page

The Purpose and Premise of Proverbs 2

The Principal Propositions in Proverbs 3

A Preview of Proverbs 5

The Power and Profit of Proverbs 7

The Providers of Proverbs 8

THE PURPOSE AND PREMISE OF PROVERBS (1:1-9)

I. The Purpose of Proverbs — To Motivate and Equip Us:

A. To Obtain Wisdom

1:1   The proverbs of Solomon the son of David,
king of Israel;

2   To know wisdom and instruction;
to perceive the words of understanding;

B. To Apply Wisdom

1:3   To receive the instruction of wisdom,
[practicing] justice, and judgment, and equity;

C. To Exercise Good Judgment

1:4   To give subtilty to the simple,
to the young man knowledge and discretion.

D. To Value Good Instruction

1:5   A wise man will hear, and will increase learning;
and a man of understanding shall attain
unto wise counsels:

E. To Search Out Truth

1:6   To understand a proverb, and the interpretation;
the words of the wise, and their dark sayings.

II. The Premise and Promise of Proverbs — Wisdom and Knowledge Are From the Lord

A. They Proceed From the Fear of the Lord

1:7   The fear of the Lord is the beginning of knowledge:
but fools despise wisdom and instruction.

B. They Are Promoted by Godly Parental Instruction

1:8   My son, hear the instruction of thy father,
and forsake not the law of thy mother:

C. They Produce a Bountiful, Rewarding Life

1:9   For they shall be an ornament of grace
unto thy head,
and chains about thy neck.

THE PRINCIPAL PROPOSITIONS IN PROVERBS
Presented By Two Opposing Life-Styles (1:10-33)

I. The Enticement of Self-Gratifying Folly

A. Its Perverse Proposition

1:10 My son, if sinners entice thee,
      consent thou not.
  11 If they say, Come with us,
        let us lay wait for blood,
        let us lurk privily for the innocent without cause:
  12 Let us swallow them up alive as the grave;
        and whole, as those that go down into the pit:

B. Its Tempting Promise

1:13 We shall find all precious substance,
      we shall fill our houses with spoil:
  14 Cast in thy lot among us;
        let us all have one purse:

C. Its Destructive Path

1:15 My son, walk not thou in the way with them;
      refrain thy foot from their path:
  16 For their feet run to evil,
        and make haste to shed blood.

D. Its Fatal Prospect

1:17 Surely in vain the net is spread
      in the sight of any bird.
  18 And they lay wait for their own blood;
        they lurk privily for their own lives.
  19 So are the ways of every one that is greedy of gain;
        which taketh away the life of the owners thereof.

II. The Invitation of Godly Wisdom

A. Its Prolonged Proposition

1:20 Wisdom crieth without;
        she uttereth her voice in the streets:
  21 She crieth in the chief place of concourse,
          in the openings of the gates:
        in the city she uttereth her words, saying,

22   How long, ye simple ones, will ye love simplicity?
and the scorners delight in their scorning,
and fools hate knowledge?

B.   Its Simple Promise

1:23   Turn you at my reproof:
behold, I will pour out my spirit unto you,
I will make known my words unto you.

C.   Its Tragic Prediction

1:24   Because I have called, and ye refused;
I have stretched out my hand,
and no man regarded;

25   But ye have set at nought all my counsel,
and would none of my reproof:

26   I also will laugh at your calamity;
I will mock when your fear cometh;

27   When your fear cometh as desolation,
and your destruction cometh as a whirlwind;
when distress and anguish cometh upon you.

28   Then shall they call upon me, but I will not answer;
they shall seek me early, but they shall not find me:

29   For that they hated knowledge,
and did not choose the fear of the Lord:

30   They would none of my counsel:
they despised all my reproof.

31   Therefore shall they eat of the fruit
of their own way,
and be filled with their own devices.

32   For the turning away of the simple shall slay them,
and the prosperity of fools shall destroy them.

D.   Its Blessed Prospect

1:33   But whoso hearkeneth unto me shall dwell safely,
and shall be quiet from fear of evil [harm].

A PREVIEW OF PROVERBS (Chapter 2)

I. God's Prerequisite for Personal Blessing

A. Receive and Obey His Word

> 2:1　My son, if thou wilt receive my words,
> 　　　and hide my commandments with thee;

B. Pursue Godly Wisdom

> 2:2　So that thou incline thine ear unto wisdom,
> 　　　and apply thine heart to understanding;
> 3　Yea, if thou criest after knowledge,
> 　　　and liftest up thy voice for understanding;
> 4　If thou seekest her as silver,
> 　　　and searchest for her as for hid treasures;

II. God's Promise for the Earnest Believer

A. Intimate Knowledge of God Himself

> 2:5　Then shalt thou understand the fear of the Lord,
> 　　　and find the knowledge of God.

B. Wisdom for Successful Living

> 2:6　For the Lord giveth wisdom:
> 　　　out of his mouth cometh knowledge
> 　　　　and understanding.

C. Protection from Harmful Influences

> 2:7　He layeth up sound wisdom for the righteous:
> 　　　he is a buckler to them that walk uprightly.
> 8　He keepeth the paths of judgment,
> 　　　and preserveth the way of his saints.

D. Mastery in the Truly Important Areas of Life

> 2:9　Then shalt thou understand righteousness,
> 　　　　and judgment, and equity;
> 　　　yea, every good path.

III. God's Prescription for the Believer's Walk

A. Walk Wisely and Circumspectly

> 2:10　When wisdom entereth into thine heart,
> 　　　and knowledge is pleasant unto thy soul;

    11   Discretion shall preserve thee,
            understanding shall keep thee:

B. Walk Separate from Sin and Sinners

  2:12   To deliver thee from the way of the evil man,
           from the man that speaketh froward things;
    13   Who leave the paths of uprightness,
           to walk in the ways of darkness;
    14   Who rejoice to do evil,
           and delight in the frowardness of the wicked;
    15   Whose ways are crooked,
           and they froward [devious] in their paths:
    16   To deliver thee from the strange woman,
           even from the stranger which flattereth
              with her words;
    17   Which forsaketh the guide [partner] of her youth,
           and forgetteth the covenant of her God.
    18   For her house inclineth unto death,
           and her paths unto the dead.
    19   None that go unto her return again,
           neither take they hold of the paths of life.

C. Walk in Goodness and Righteousness

  2:20 That thou mayest walk in the way of good men,
           and keep the paths of the righteous.

IV. God's Provision for the Believer and Unbeliever

A. Contentment and Stability for the Faithful Believer

  2:21 For the upright shall dwell in the land,
           and the perfect shall remain in it.

B. Trouble and Destruction for the Unbeliever

  2:22 But the wicked shall be cut off from the earth,
           and the transgressors shall be rooted out of it.

THE POWER AND PROFIT OF PROVERBS

I. "All Scripture Is Given by Inspiration of God . . .

30:5 Every word of God is pure:
　　　he is a shield unto them that put their trust in him.

6 Add thou not unto his words,
　　lest he reprove thee, and thou be found a liar.

II. "And Is Profitable . . .

A. For Doctrine . . .

4:1 Hear, ye children, the instruction of a father,
　　　and attend to know understanding.

2 For I give you good doctrine,
　forsake ye not my law.

B. For Reproof . . .

1:23 Turn you at my reproof:
　　　behold, I will pour out my spirit unto you,
　　　I will make known my words unto you.

15:31 The ear that heareth the reproof of life
　　　abideth among the wise.

32 He that refuseth instruction despiseth his own soul:
　but he that heareth reproof getteth understanding.

C. For Correction . . .

3:11 My son, despise not the chastening of the Lord;
　　　neither be weary of his correction:

12 For whom the Lord loveth he correcteth;
　even as a father the son in whom he delighteth.

D. For Instruction in Righteousness . . .

8:6 Hear; for I will speak of excellent things;
　　and the opening of my lips shall be right things.

7 For my mouth shall speak truth;
　and wickedness is an abomination to my lips.

8 All the words of my mouth are in righteousness;
　there is nothing froward or perverse in them.

9 They are all plain to him that understandeth,
　and right to them that find knowledge.

III. **"That the Man of God May Be . . .**

    A. Perfect . . .

      11:5 The righteousness of the perfect shall direct his way:
             but the wicked shall fall by his own wickedness.

      2:21 For the upright shall dwell in the land,
             and the perfect shall remain in it.

    B. Throughly Furnished Unto All Good Works"
       (II Tim. 3:16-17)

      10:16 The labour of the righteous tendeth to life:
              the fruit of the wicked to sin.

      21:8 The way of man is froward and strange:
             but as for the pure, his work is right.

      11:30 The fruit of the righteous is a tree of life;
              and he that winneth souls is wise.

THE PROVIDERS OF PROVERBS
"Holy Men of God Spake as They Were Moved
by the Holy Ghost" (I Pet. 1:21)

I. **Solomon**

    A. Chapters 1–22:16

      1:1 The proverbs of Solomon the son of David,
          king of Israel;

      10:1 The proverbs of Solomon.
           A wise son maketh a glad father:
           but a foolish son is the heaviness of his mother.

    B. Chapters 25-29

      25:1 These are also proverbs of Solomon,
           which the men of Hezekiah king of Judah copied out.

II. **Unidentified Wise Men** (Possibly Solomon)

      Chapters 22:17–24:34

      22:17 Bow down thine ear, and hear the words of the wise,
           and apply thine heart unto my knowledge.

24:23 These things also belong to the wise.
It is not good to have respect of persons in judgment.

III. **Agur** (Not named in Scripture other than in 30:1)

Chapter 30

30:1 The words of Agur the son of Jakeh,
even the prophecy:
the man spake unto Ithiel, even unto Ithiel
and Ucal,

IV. **Lemuel** (Not named in Scripture other than in 31:1 and 31:4)

Chapter 31

31:1 The words of king Lemuel,
the prophecy that his mother taught him.

Chapter 2

The Almighty God — Our Father

The fear of the Lord is the beginning of wisdom:
and the knowledge of the Holy [One] is understanding.

(9:10)

                                                                    Page

God's Power and Sovereignty 12

God's Wisdom..13

God's Delights and Displeasures........................15

God's Actions and Responses 17

God's Word 21

GOD'S POWER AND SOVEREIGNTY

I. God Created All Things

A.   The Universe and Nature

3:19   The Lord by wisdom hath founded the earth;
by understanding hath he established the heavens.

20   By his knowledge the depths are broken up,
and the clouds drop down the dew.

30:4   Who hath ascended up into heaven, or descended?
who hath gathered the wind in his fists?
who hath bound the waters in a garment?
who hath established all the ends of the earth?
what is his name, and what is his son's name,
if thou canst tell?

26:10   The great God that formed all things
both rewardeth the fool, and rewardeth transgressors.

B.   All People and Their Capabilities

22:2   The rich and poor meet together [in common]:
the Lord is the maker of them all.

29:13   The poor and the deceitful man meet together:
the Lord lighteneth both their eyes.

20:12   The hearing ear, and the seeing eye,
the Lord hath made even both of them.

C.   All Creatures and Their Characteristics

30:18   There be three things which are too wonderful for me,
yea, four which I know not:

19   The way of an eagle in the air;
the way of a serpent upon a rock;
the way of a ship in the midst of the sea;
and the way of a man with a maid.

30:24   There be four things which are little upon the earth,
but they are exceeding wise:

25   The ants are a people not strong,
yet they prepare their meat in the summer;

26   The conies [badgers] are but a feeble folk,
yet make they their houses in the rocks;

27 The locusts have no king,
   yet go they forth all of them by bands;
28 The spider taketh hold with her hands,
   and is in kings' palaces.

II. **God Has a Purpose for All Things**

16:4 The Lord hath made all things for himself:
   yea, even the wicked for the day of evil.

III. **God Controls All Things**

A. The Activities of Nations and Rulers

21:1 The king's heart is in the hand of the Lord,
   as the rivers of water:
   he turneth it whithersoever he will.

16:10 A divine sentence is in the lips of the king:
   his mouth transgresseth not in judgment.

21:31 The horse is prepared against the day of battle:
   but safety [victory] is of the Lord.

B. The Words and Deeds of Individuals

20:24 Man's goings are of the Lord;
   how can a man then understand his own way?

16:1 The preparations of the heart in man,
   and the answer of the tongue, is from the Lord.

16:9 A man's heart deviseth his way:
   but the Lord directeth his steps.

C. The Outcome of Every Matter

16:33 The lot is cast into the lap;
   but the whole disposing thereof is of the Lord.

GOD'S WISDOM

I. **God's Wisdom Is Beyond Human Comprehension**

A. "As the Heavens Are Higher Than the Earth, . . .

3:19 The Lord by wisdom hath founded the earth;
   by understanding hath he established the heavens.

B. So Are My Ways Higher Than Your Ways, . . .

25:2   It is the glory of God to conceal a thing:
      but the honour of kings is to search out a matter.

30:2   Surely I am more brutish than any man,
      and have not the understanding of a man.
   3   I neither learned wisdom,
      nor have the knowledge of the holy [Holy One].

C. And My Thoughts Higher Than Your Thoughts" (Isa. 55:9)

19:21   There are many devices in a man's heart;
       nevertheless the counsel of the Lord, that shall stand.

22:30   There is no wisdom nor understanding nor counsel
       against the Lord.

II. Christ Is "God's Wisdom" Revealed to Men (8:22-36)

A. "In the Beginning . . . the Word Was With God . . .

8:22   The Lord possessed me in the beginning of his way,
      before his works of old.

B. And the Word Was God."

8:23   I was set up from everlasting,
      from the beginning, or ever the earth was.
  24   When there were no depths, I was brought forth;
      when there were no fountains abounding with water.
  25   Before the mountains were settled,
      before the hills was I brought forth:
  26   While as yet he had not made the earth, nor the fields,
      nor the highest part of the dust of the world.

C. "Without Him Was Not Any Thing Made That Was Made."

8:27   When he prepared the heavens, I was there:
      when he set a compass upon the face of the depth:
  28   When he established the clouds above:
      when he strengthened the fountains of the deep:
  29   When he gave to the sea his decree,
      that the waters should not pass his commandment:
      when he appointed the foundations of the earth:

D. "In Him Was Life [Perfect Fellowship With God]; . . .

8:30 Then I was by him, as one brought up with him:
and I was daily his delight,
rejoicing always before him;

E. And the Life Was the Light of Men."
(Christ Gives Life to Men)

8:31 Rejoicing in the habitable part of his earth;
and my delights were with the sons of men.

F. "As Many as Received Him, . . ."

8:32 Now therefore hearken unto me, O ye children:
for blessed are they that keep my ways.
33 Hear instruction, and be wise, and refuse it not.
34 Blessed is the man that heareth me,
watching daily at my gates,
waiting at the posts of my doors.

G. Gave He Power to Become the Sons of God" (John 1:1-12)

8:35 For whoso findeth me findeth life,
and shall obtain favour of the Lord.

H. "But He That Believeth Not Is Condemned Already . . ."
(John 3:18)

8:36 But he that sinneth against me wrongeth his own soul:
all they that hate me love death.

GOD'S DELIGHTS AND DISPLEASURES

I. Traits and Deeds That Delight God

A. Righteous (vs. Wicked) Lives

15:9 The way of the wicked is an abomination
unto the Lord:
but he loveth him that followeth after righteousness.

11:20 They that are of a froward heart are abomination
to the Lord:
but such as are upright in their way are his delight.

3:31 Envy thou not the oppressor,
and choose none of his ways.

32   For the froward is abomination to the Lord:
  but his secret is with the righteous.

21:3   To do justice and judgment is more acceptable
  to the Lord than sacrifice.

B.   Pure (vs. Impure) Thoughts and Words

15:26   The thoughts of the wicked are an abomination
  to the Lord:
  but the words of the pure are pleasant words.

12:22   Lying lips are abomination to the Lord:
  but they that deal truly are his delight.

C.   Acceptable (vs. Unacceptable) Worship and Prayer

15:8   The sacrifice of the wicked is an abomination
  to the Lord:
  but the prayer of the upright is his delight.

21:27   The sacrifice of the wicked is abomination:
  how much more, when he bringeth it with a
  wicked mind?

28:9   He that turneth away his ear from hearing the law,
  even his prayer shall be abomination.

D.   Honest (vs. Dishonest) Dealing

11:1   A false balance is abomination to the Lord:
  but a just weight is his delight.

16:11   A just weight and balance are the Lord's:
  all the weights of the bag are his work.

20:10   Divers weights, and divers measures,
  both of them are alike abomination to the Lord.

20:23   Divers weights are an abomination unto the Lord;
  and a false balance is not good.

II. Traits and Deeds That Displease God

A.   A Proud Spirit

16:5   Every one that is proud in heart is an abomination
  to the Lord:
  though hand join in hand,
   he shall not be unpunished.

B. Injustice and False Accusations

17:15 He that justifieth the wicked,
and he that condemneth the just,
even they both are abomination to the Lord.

C. Sexual Immorality

22:14 The mouth of strange women is a deep pit:
he that is abhorred of the Lord shall fall therein.

D. Joy Over Another's Trouble

24:17 Rejoice not when thine enemy falleth,
and let not thine heart be glad
when he stumbleth:
18 Lest the Lord see it, and it displease him,
and he turn away his wrath from him.

E. Wrong Attitudes, Evil Actions, and Lies

6:16 These six things doth the Lord hate:
yea, seven are an abomination unto him:
17 A proud look,
a lying tongue,
and hands that shed innocent blood,
18 An heart that deviseth wicked imaginations,
feet that be swift in running to mischief,
19 A false witness that speaketh lies,
and he that soweth discord among brethren.

GOD'S ACTIONS AND RESPONSES

I. He Observes and Judges All Men

A. He Sees All Acts and Deeds

15:3 The eyes of the Lord are in every place,
beholding the evil and the good.
5:21 For the ways of man are before the eyes of the Lord,
and he pondereth all his goings.

B. He Knows All Thoughts and Motives

21:2 Every way of a man is right in his own eyes:
but the Lord pondereth the hearts.

16:2   All the ways of a man are clean in his own eyes;
  but the Lord weigheth the spirits [motives].

15:11   Hell and destruction are before the Lord:
  how much more then the hearts
   of the children of men?

17:3   The fining pot is for silver,
  and the furnace for gold:
  but the Lord trieth the hearts.

20:27   The spirit of man is the candle of the Lord,
  searching all the inward parts of the belly.

C. He Sees Through All Excuses

24:11   If thou forbear to deliver them that are
   drawn unto death,
  and those that are ready to be slain;

12   If thou sayest, Behold, we knew it not;
  doth not he that pondereth the heart consider it?
  and he that keepeth thy soul, doth not he know it?
  and shall not he render to every man according
   to his works?

D. He Judges All Men Justly

29:26   Many seek the ruler's favour;
  but every man's judgment cometh from the Lord.

II. He Blesses the Righteous and Condemns the Wicked

12:2   A good man obtaineth favour of the Lord:
  but a man of wicked devices will he condemn.

3:33   The curse of the Lord is in the house of the wicked:
  but he blesseth the habitation of the just.

34   Surely he scorneth the scorners:
  but he giveth grace unto the lowly.

III. He Has an Intimate Relationship With His Own

A. He Reveals His Will to Them

3:32   For the froward is abomination to the Lord:
  but his secret is with the righteous.

B. He Answers Their Prayers

  15:29 The Lord is far from the wicked:
        but he heareth the prayer of the righteous.

C. He Disciplines Them in Love

  3:11 My son, despise not the chastening of the Lord;
        neither be weary of his correction:
    12 For whom the Lord loveth he correcteth;
        even as a father the son in whom he delighteth.

D. He Forgives Their Confessed Sin

  16:6 By mercy and truth iniquity is purged:
        and by the fear of the Lord men depart from evil.

IV. **He Guides and Protects His Own**

A. He Gives Them Wisdom and Direction

  2:6 For the Lord giveth wisdom:
      out of his mouth cometh knowledge
        and understanding.

  3:6 In all thy ways acknowledge him,
      and he shall direct thy paths.

B. He Protects Them From Harm

  2:7 He layeth up sound wisdom for the righteous:
      he is a buckler to them that walk uprightly.
    8 He keepeth the paths of judgment,
      and preserveth the way of his saints.

  3:25 Be not afraid of sudden fear,
      neither of the desolation of the wicked,
        when it cometh.
    26 For the Lord shall be thy confidence,
      and shall keep thy foot from being taken.

  16:7 When a man's ways please the Lord,
      he maketh even his enemies to be at peace with him.

C. He Provides for All Their Needs

  10:3 The Lord will not suffer the soul of the righteous
        to famish:
      but he casteth away the substance of the wicked.

V. **He Rewards Kindness Toward Others**

A. He Repays Generosity Shown to the Needy

19:17   He that hath pity upon the poor lendeth
   unto the Lord;
  and that which he hath given will he
   pay him again.

B. He Rewards Kindness Shown to Enemies

25:21   If thine enemy be hungry, give him bread to eat;
  and if he be thirsty, give him water to drink:
 22   For thou shalt heap coals of fire upon his head,
  and the Lord shall reward thee.

VI. **He Defends and Upholds the Mistreated**

A. He Protects the Disadvantaged

22:22   Rob not the poor, because he is poor:
  neither oppress the afflicted in the gate:
 23   For the Lord will plead their cause,
  and spoil the soul of those that spoiled them.

23:10   Remove not the old landmark;
  and enter not into the fields of the fatherless:
 11   For their redeemer is mighty;
  he shall plead their cause with thee.

22:28   Remove not the ancient landmark,
  which thy fathers have set.

15:25   The Lord will destroy the house of the proud:
  but he will establish the border of the widow.

B. He Delivers the Innocent and Avenges Injustices

20:22   Say not thou, I will recompense evil;
  but wait on the Lord, and he shall save thee.

VII. **He Thwarts and Defeats Sinners**

22:12   The eyes of the Lord preserve knowledge,
  and he overthroweth the words of the transgressor.

21:12   The righteous man wisely considereth the house
of the wicked:
but God overthroweth the wicked
for their wickedness.

GOD'S WORD

I. God's Word Is Perfect and Complete

30:5   Every word of God is pure:
he is a shield unto them that put their trust in him.

6   Add thou not unto his words,
lest he reprove thee, and thou be found a liar.

II. God's Word Must Be Obeyed

A.   Obedience Is a Matter of Life or Death

19:16   He that keepeth the commandment keepeth
his own soul;
but he that despiseth his ways shall die.

13:13   Whoso despiseth the word shall be destroyed:
but he that feareth the commandment
shall be rewarded.

B.   Obedience Brings Wisdom

28:7   Whoso keepeth the law is a wise son:
but he that is a companion of riotous men
shameth his father.

C.   Obedience Brings True Happiness

29:18   Where there is no vision, the people perish:
but he that keepeth the law, happy is he.

D.   Obedience Rebukes the Disobedience of Others

28:4   They that forsake the law praise the wicked:
but such as keep the law contend with them.

E.   Disobedience Precludes Effective Prayer

28:9   He that turneth away his ear from hearing the law,
even his prayer shall be abomination.

III. **God's Law Is "My Law"; Make It "Your Law"**

A.   It Leads to a Close Relationship With God

2:1   My son, if thou wilt receive my words,
    and hide my commandments with thee;

2   So that thou incline thine ear unto wisdom,
    and apply thine heart to understanding;

3   Yea, if thou criest after knowledge,
    and liftest up thy voice for understanding;

4   If thou seekest her as silver,
    and searchest for her as for hid treasures;

5   Then shalt thou understand the fear of the Lord,
    and find the knowledge of God.

B.   It Teaches Sound Doctrine and Principles for Living

4:1   Hear, ye children, the instruction of a father,
    and attend to know understanding.

2   For I give you good doctrine,
    forsake ye not my law.

3   For I was my father's son,
    tender and only beloved in the sight of my mother.

4   He taught me also, and said unto me,
    Let thine heart retain my words:
    keep my commandments, and live.

7:1   My son, keep my words,
    and lay up my commandments with thee.

2   Keep my commandments, and live;
    and my law as the apple of thine eye.

3   Bind them upon thy fingers,
    write them upon the table of thine heart.

C.   It Strengthens Faith in God

22:17   Bow down thine ear, and hear the words of the wise,
    and apply thine heart unto my knowledge.

18   For it is a pleasant thing if thou keep them
      within thee;
    they shall withal be fitted [be ready] in thy lips.

19   That thy trust may be in the Lord,
    I have made known to thee this day, even to thee.

20   Have not I written to thee excellent things
    in counsels and knowledge,

21   That I might make thee know the certainty of
the words of truth;
that thou mightest answer the words of truth
to them that send unto thee?

D.   It Offers an Abundant Life

1:8   My son, hear the instruction of thy father,
and forsake not the law of thy mother:

9   For they shall be an ornament of grace
unto thy head,
and chains about thy neck.

3:1   My son, forget not my law;
but let thine heart keep my commandments:

2   For length of days, and long life, and peace,
shall they add to thee.

E.   It Provides Guidance and Protection Against Sin

6:20   My son, keep thy father's commandment,
and forsake not the law of thy mother:

21   Bind them continually upon thine heart,
and tie them about thy neck.

22   When thou goest, it shall lead thee;
when thou sleepest, it shall keep thee;
and when thou awakest, it shall talk with thee.

23   For the commandment is a lamp;
and the law is light;
and reproofs of instruction are the way of life:

24   To keep thee from the evil woman,
from the flattery of the tongue of a strange woman.

Chapter 3

Life or Death — Everyone's Choice

In the way of righteousness is life;
and in the pathway thereof there is no death.

(12:28)

Page

The Fear of the Lord 26

True Life 28

Death 30

Sowing and Reaping 34

THE FEAR OF THE LORD
(Reverence and Submission Before God)

I. The Fear of the Lord Is the Basis of True Life

A. The Source of Refreshing Spiritual Life

14:27 The fear of the Lord is a fountain of life,
to depart from the snares of death.

B. The Foundation of Wisdom and Knowledge

9:10 The fear of the Lord is the beginning of wisdom:
and the knowledge of the holy is understanding.

11 For by me thy days shall be multiplied,
and the years of thy life shall be increased.

15:33 The fear of the Lord is the instruction of wisdom;
and before honour is humility.

1:7 The fear of the Lord is the beginning of knowledge:
but fools despise wisdom and instruction.

C. A Prerequisite of All That Is Worthwhile in Life

1. Happiness and Contentment

28:14 Happy is the man that feareth alway:
but he that hardeneth his heart shall fall
into mischief.

15:16 Better is little with the fear of the Lord
than great treasure and trouble therewith.

2. Peace and Security

19:23 The fear of the Lord tendeth to life:
and he that hath it shall abide satisfied;
he shall not be visited with evil.

14:26 In the fear of the Lord is strong confidence:
and his children shall have a place of refuge.

3. Physical Well-Being

3:7 Be not wise in thine own eyes:
fear the Lord, and depart from evil.

8 It shall be health to thy navel,
and marrow to thy bones.

10:27 The fear of the Lord prolongeth days:
      but the years of the wicked shall be shortened.

  4. Material Blessings and Honor

22:4 By humility and the fear of the Lord
      are riches, and honour, and life.

31:30 Favour is deceitful, and beauty is vain:
      but a woman that feareth the Lord,
        she shall be praised.

II. The Fear of the Lord Is Manifested by a Holy Life

  A. Upright Conduct

14:2 He that walketh in his uprightness
      feareth the Lord:
      but he that is perverse in his ways despiseth him.

  B. Separation From Evil

8:13 The fear of the Lord is to hate evil:
      pride, and arrogancy, and the evil way,
      and the froward mouth, do I hate.

14:16 A wise man feareth, and departeth from evil:
      but the fool rageth, and is confident.

16:6 By mercy and truth iniquity is purged:
      and by the fear of the Lord men depart from evil.

  C. Separation From the Wrong Kind of People

24:21 My son, fear thou the Lord and the king:
      and meddle not with them that are given to change:
  22 For their calamity shall rise suddenly;
      and who knoweth the ruin of them both?

23:17 Let not thine heart envy sinners:
      but be thou in the fear of the Lord all the day long.
  18 For surely there is an end;
      and thine expectation shall not be cut off.

III. The Fear of the Lord Increases Through Discovery of God's Truth

2:1 My son, if thou wilt receive my words,
      and hide my commandments with thee;

2   So that thou incline thine ear unto wisdom,
    and apply thine heart to understanding; . . .
5   Then shalt thou understand the fear of the Lord,
    and find the knowledge of God.

IV. Refusing to Fear the Lord Brings Trouble and Judgment

1:29   For that they hated knowledge,
    and did not choose the fear of the Lord:
30   They would none of my counsel:
    they despised all my reproof.
31   Therefore shall they eat of the fruit
      of their own way,
    and be filled with their own devices.
32   For the turning away of the simple shall slay them,
    and the prosperity of fools shall destroy them.

TRUE LIFE
(God's Prescription for True Life)

I. Fear the Lord (In Reverence and Submission)

14:27   The fear of the Lord is a fountain of life,
    to depart from the snares of death.

22:4   By humility and the fear of the Lord
    are riches, and honour, and life.

II. Practice God's Righteousness

21:21   He that followeth after righteousness and mercy
    findeth life, righteousness, and honour.

11:19   As righteousness tendeth to life:
    so he that pursueth evil pursueth it
      to his own death.

12:28   In the way of righteousness is life;
    and in the pathway thereof there is no death.

10:16   The labour of the righteous tendeth to life:
    the fruit of the wicked to sin.

III. Obey Godly Instruction

10:17   He is in the way of life that keepeth instruction:
  but he that refuseth reproof erreth.

4:20   My son, attend to my words;
  incline thine ear unto my sayings. . . .

22   For they are life unto those that find them,
  and health to all their flesh.

4:4   He taught me also, and said unto me,
  Let thine heart retain my words:
  keep my commandments, and live.

7:2   Keep my commandments, and live;
  and my law as the apple of thine eye.

IV. Pursue Wisdom and Understanding

13:14   The law of the wise is a fountain of life,
  to depart from the snares of death.

15:24   The way of life is above to the wise,
  that he may depart from hell beneath.

3:21   My son, let not them depart from thine eyes:
  keep sound wisdom and discretion:

22   So shall they be life unto thy soul,
  and grace to thy neck.

8:35   For whoso findeth me findeth life,
  and shall obtain favour of the Lord.

16:22   Understanding is a wellspring of life unto him
  that hath it:
  but the instruction of fools is folly.

9:6   Forsake the foolish, and live;
  and go in the way of understanding.

3:18   She is a tree of life to them that lay hold upon her:
  and happy is every one that retaineth her.

V. Practice Self-Control

A.   Of Thoughts and Desires

4:23   Keep thy heart with all diligence;
  for out of it are the issues of life.

14:30   A sound heart is the life of the flesh:
      but envy the rottenness of the bones.

B. Of Words and Speech

13:3   He that keepeth his mouth keepeth his life:
      but he that openeth wide his lips
        shall have destruction.

18:21   Death and life are in the power of the tongue:
      and they that love it shall eat the fruit thereof.

15:4   A wholesome tongue is a tree of life:
      but perverseness therein is a breach in the spirit.

VI. Please Those in Authority

16:15   In the light of the king's countenance is life;
      and his favour is as a cloud of the latter rain.

VII. Share True Life With Others

11:30   The fruit of the righteous is a tree of life;
      and he that winneth souls is wise.

10:11   The mouth of a righteous man is a well of life:
      but violence covereth the mouth of the wicked.

DEATH

I. Physical Death

A. Everyone Faces Eventual Death

27:20   Hell [the grave] and destruction are never full;
      so the eyes of man are never satisfied.

30:15   The horseleach hath two daughters,
          crying, Give, give.
      There are three things that are never satisfied,
      yea, four things say not, It is enough.

16   The grave; and the barren womb;
      the earth that is not filled with water;
      and the fire that saith not, It is enough.

B. Believers Look Expectantly Beyond Death

14:32   The wicked is driven away in his wickedness:
   but the righteous hath hope in his death.

C. Unbelievers Are Unprepared for Death

16:25   There is a way that seemeth right unto a man,
   but the end thereof are the ways of death.

11:7   When a wicked man dieth,
   his expectation shall perish:
  and the hope of unjust men perisheth.

D. The Wicked Invite Premature Death

10:27   The fear of the Lord prolongeth days:
   but the years of the wicked shall be shortened.

2:21   For the upright shall dwell in the land,
   and the perfect shall remain in it.
22   But the wicked shall be cut off from the earth,
   and the transgressors shall be rooted out of it.

II. Spiritual Death

A. Unbelievers Are Already Spiritually Dead

21:16   The man that wandereth out of the way
   of understanding
  shall remain in the congregation of the dead.

29:18   Where there is no vision, the people perish:
   but he that keepeth the law, happy is he.

B. Believers Are Delivered From Spiritual Death

14:27   The fear of the Lord is a fountain of life,
   to depart from the snares of death.

12:28   In the way of righteousness is life;
   and in the pathway thereof there is no death.

10:2   Treasures of wickedness profit nothing:
   but righteousness delivereth from death.

13:14   The law of the wise is a fountain of life,
   to depart from the snares of death.

II. "Living Death" (The Godless Life That Leads to Eternal Death)

A. Its Basic Cause

1. Spiritual Foolishness and Indifference

10:21   The lips of the righteous feed many:
          but fools die for want of wisdom.

19:16   He that keepeth the commandment keepeth
              his own soul;
          but he that despiseth his ways shall die.

9:18   But he [the naive] knoweth not that the dead
              are there;
          and that her guests [fools] are in the depths of hell.

2. Refusal of Correction

15:10   Correction is grievous unto him that
              forsaketh the way:
          and he that hateth reproof shall die.

29:1   He, that being often reproved hardeneth his neck,
              shall suddenly be destroyed, and that
              without remedy.

3. Rejection of God's Salvation

8:35   For whoso findeth me findeth life,
              and shall obtain favour of the Lord.

36   But he that sinneth against me
              wrongeth his own soul:
          and they that hate me love death.

B. Its Evidence

1. Deliberate Practice of Sin

11:19   As righteousness tendeth to life:
          so he that pursueth evil pursueth it
              to his own death.

5:22   His own iniquities shall take the wicked himself,
              and he shall be holden with the cords of his sins.

23   He shall die without instruction;
          and in the greatness of his folly he shall go astray.

2. Corrupt and Deceitful Speech

18:21 Death and life are in the power of the tongue:
and they that love it shall eat the fruit thereof.

21:6 The getting of treasures by a lying tongue
is a vanity tossed to and fro of them that
seek death.

3. Sexual Immorality

6:32 But whoso committeth adultery with a woman
lacketh understanding:
he that doeth it destroyeth his own soul.

7:26 For she hath cast down many wounded:
yea, many strong men have been slain by her.

27 Her house is the way to hell,
going down to the chambers of death.

2:18 For her house inclineth unto death,
and her paths unto the dead.

19 None that go unto her return again,
neither take they hold of the paths of life.

4. Violence and Crime

1:10 My son, if sinners entice thee,
consent thou not.

11 If they say, Come with us, let us lay wait for blood,
let us lurk privily for the innocent without cause:

12 Let us swallow them up alive as the grave;
and whole, as those that go down into the pit:

13 We shall find all precious substance,
we shall fill our houses with spoil: . . .

18 . . . they lay wait for their own blood;
they lurk privily for their own lives.

19 So are the ways of every one that is greedy of gain;
which taketh away the life of the owners thereof.

28:17 A man that doeth violence to the blood of any person
shall flee to the pit;
let no man stay him.

SOWING AND REAPING

I. **We All Reap What We Sow — Whether Good or Bad**

A. We Will Be Repaid for All of Our Works

24:12   If thou sayest, Behold, we knew it not;
doth not he that pondereth the heart consider it?
and he that keepeth thy soul, doth not he know it?
and shall not he render to every man
according to his works?

12:14   A man shall be satisfied with good
by the fruit of his mouth:
and the recompence of a man's hands
shall be rendered unto him.

11:18   The wicked worketh a deceitful work:
but to him that soweth righteousness
shall be a sure reward.

B. We Will Be Repaid in Like Kind

13:21   Evil pursueth sinners:
but to the righteous good shall be repayed.

11:27   He that diligently seeketh good procureth favour:
but he that seeketh mischief, it shall come unto him.

C. We Will Be Repaid in Full

14:14   The backslider in heart shall be filled with his
own ways:
and a good man shall be satisfied from himself.

22:8   He that soweth iniquity shall reap vanity:
and the rod of his anger shall fail.

D. We Will Be Repaid in This Life

11:31   Behold, the righteous shall be recompensed
in the earth:
much more the wicked and the sinner.

11:25   The liberal soul shall be made fat:
and he that watereth shall be watered also himself.

E. We Will Be Repaid in Eternity

  10:24 The fear of the wicked, it shall come upon him:
        but the desire of the righteous shall be granted.
     25 As the whirlwind passeth, so is the wicked no more:
        but the righteous is an everlasting foundation.

II. The Sinner Reaps His Own Wrong-Doing

A. His Sins Will Trap and Entangle Him

  5:22 His own iniquities shall take the wicked himself,
      and he shall be holden with the cords of his sins.

  12:13 The wicked is snared by the transgression of his lips:
      but the just shall come out of trouble.

  11:6 The righteousness of the upright shall deliver them:
      but transgressors shall be taken in their
        own naughtiness.

B. His Sins Will Subvert and Afflict Him

  26:27 Whoso diggeth a pit shall fall therein:
      and he that rolleth a stone, it will return upon him.

  28:10 Whoso causeth the righteous to go astray
        in an evil way,
      he shall fall himself into his own pit:
      but the upright shall have good things in possession.

C. His Sins Will Destroy Him

  1:30 They would none of my counsel:
      they despised all my reproof.
    31 Therefore shall they eat of the fruit
        of their own way,
      and be filled with their own devices.
    32 For the turning away of the simple shall slay them,
      and the prosperity of fools shall destroy them.

Chapter 4

The True Believer

Trust in the Lord with all thine heart;
and lean not unto thine own understanding.
In all thy ways acknowledge Him,
and He shall direct thy paths.

(3:5-6)

                                                                    Page

The Believer's Priorities 38

The Believer's Objectives 40

The Believer's Life 43

The Believer's Blessings 45

The Believer's Protection 47

THE BELIEVER'S PRIORITIES (Chapter 4)

I. Learning God's Word

4:1   Hear, ye children, the instruction of a father,
and attend to know understanding.

2   For I give you good doctrine,
forsake ye not my law.

3   For I was my father's son,
tender and only beloved in the sight of my mother.

4   He taught me also, and said unto me,
Let thine heart retain my words:
keep my commandments, and live.

II. Obtaining Godly Wisdom

4:5   Get wisdom, get understanding: forget it not;
neither decline from the words of my mouth.

6   Forsake her not, and she shall preserve thee:
love her, and she shall keep thee.

7   Wisdom is the principal thing; therefore get wisdom:
and with all thy getting get understanding.

8   Exalt her, and she shall promote thee:
she shall bring thee to honour,
when thou dost embrace her.

9   She shall give to thine head an ornament of grace:
a crown of glory shall she deliver to thee.

III. Practicing Godly Living

4:10   Hear, O my son, and receive my sayings;
and the years of thy life shall be many.

11   I have taught thee in the way of wisdom;
I have led thee in right paths.

12   When thou goest, thy steps shall not be straitened;
and when thou runnest, thou shalt not stumble.

13   Take fast hold of instruction;
let her not go: keep her; for she is thy life.

IV. Avoiding Sinful Influences

4:14   Enter not into the path of the wicked,
and go not in the way of evil men.

15   Avoid it, pass not by it,
    turn from it, and pass away.
16   For they sleep not, except they have done mischief;
    and their sleep is taken away,
    unless they cause some to fall.
17   For they eat the bread of wickedness,
    and drink the wine of violence.

V. Achieving Spiritual Growth

4:18   But the path of the just is as the shining light,
    that shineth more and more unto the perfect day.
19   The way of the wicked is as darkness:
    they know not at what they stumble.

VI. Following God's Direction

4:20   My son, attend to my words;
    incline thine ear unto my sayings.
21   Let them not depart from thine eyes;
    keep them in the midst of thine heart.
22   For they are life unto those that find them,
    and health to all their flesh.

VII. Exercising Self-Discipline

4:23   Keep thy heart with all diligence;
    for out of it are the issues of life.
24   Put away from thee a froward mouth,
    and perverse lips put far from thee.
25   Let thine eyes look right on,
    and let thine eyelids look straight before thee.
26   Ponder the path of thy feet,
    and let all thy ways be established.
27   Turn not to the right hand nor to the left:
    remove thy foot from evil.

THE BELIEVER'S OBJECTIVES (Chapter 3)

I. A Close, Personal Relationship With God

A. Willing Obedience to God's Word

3:1   My son, forget not my law;
but let thine heart keep my commandments:

2   For length of days, and long life, and peace,
shall they add to thee.

B. Development of God-Like Character

3:3   Let not mercy and truth forsake thee:
bind them about thy neck;
write them upon the table of thine heart:

4   So shalt thou find favour and good understanding
in the sight of God and man.

C. Total Commitment to God

3:5   Trust in the Lord with all thine heart;
and lean not unto thine own understanding.

6   In all thy ways acknowledge him,
and he shall direct thy paths.

II. Faithful Application of God-Given Principles

A. Godly Humility and Holy Living

3:7   Be not wise in thine own eyes:
fear the Lord, and depart from evil.

8   It shall be health to thy navel,
and marrow to thy bones.

B. Faithful Stewardship of Material Possessions

3:9   Honour the Lord with thy substance,
and with the firstfruits of all thine increase:

10   So shall thy barns be filled with plenty,
and thy presses shall burst out with new wine.

C. Proper Acceptance of God's Discipline

3:11   My son, despise not the chastening of the Lord;
neither be weary of his correction:

12   For whom the Lord loveth he correcteth;
even as a father the son in whom he delighteth.

III. **A Godly Perspective on Life**

  A. Seeking Godly Wisdom as First Priority

    3:13 Happy is the man that findeth wisdom,
           and the man that getteth understanding.
      14 For the merchandise of it is better than
           the merchandise of silver,
           and the gain thereof than fine gold.
      15 She is more precious than rubies:
           and all the things thou canst desire
             are not to be compared unto her.

  B. Valuing the Results and Benefits of Wisdom

    3:16 Length of days is in her right hand;
           and in her left hand riches and honour.
      17 Her ways are ways of pleasantness,
           and all her paths are peace.
      18 She is a tree of life to them that lay hold upon her:
           and happy is every one that retaineth her.

  C. Acknowledging God's Power and Sovereignty

    3:19 The Lord by wisdom hath founded the earth;
           by understanding hath he established the heavens.
      20 By his knowledge the depths are broken up,
           and the clouds drop down the dew.

IV. **Dependence on God for Daily Living**

  A. Ability to Meet Life's Challenges and Avoid Its Pitfalls

    3:21 My son, let not them depart from thine eyes:
           keep sound wisdom and discretion:
      22 So shall they be life unto thy soul,
           and grace to thy neck.
      23 Then shalt thou walk in thy way safely,
           and thy foot shall not stumble.

  B. Protection From External Sources of Harm

    3:24 When thou liest down, thou shalt not be afraid:
           yea, thou shalt lie down, and thy sleep
             shall be sweet.

25 Be not afraid of sudden fear,
    neither of the desolation [attack] of the wicked,
        when it cometh.
26 For the Lord shall be thy confidence,
    and shall keep thy foot from being taken.

V. Wholesome Relationships With Others

  A. Faithful Service to Others

    3:27 Withhold not good from them to whom it is due,
        when it is in the power of thine hand to do it.
     28 Say not unto thy neighbour, Go, and come again,
        and tomorrow I will give;
        when thou hast it by thee.

  B. Peaceful Relationships With Others

    3:29 Devise not evil against thy neighbour,
        seeing he dwelleth securely by thee.
     30 Strive not with a man without cause,
        if he have done thee no harm.

  C. Separation From the Ungodly

    3:31 Envy thou not the oppressor,
        and choose none of his ways.
     32 For the froward is abomination to the Lord:
        but his secret is with the righteous.

VI. God's Blessing and Reward — In This Life and Beyond

    3:33 The curse of the Lord is in the house of the wicked:
        but he blesseth the habitation of the just.
     34 Surely he scorneth the scorners:
        but he giveth grace unto the lowly.
     35 The wise shall inherit glory:
        but shame shall be the promotion of fools.

THE BELIEVER'S LIFE

I. The Believer Lives by God-Given Principles

A. He Is Guided by Godly Principles

11:5   The righteousness of the perfect shall direct his way:
but the wicked shall fall by his own wickedness.

13:6   Righteousness keepeth him that is upright
in the way:
but wickedness overthroweth the sinner.

11:3   The integrity of the upright shall guide them:
but the perverseness of transgressors
shall destroy them.

21:8   The way of man is froward and strange:
but as for the pure, his work is right.

B. He Is Strengthened by Godly Principles

10:29   The way of the Lord is strength to the upright:
but destruction shall be to the workers of iniquity.

28:1   The wicked flee when no man pursueth:
but the righteous are bold as a lion.

24:16   For a just man falleth seven times,
and riseth up again:
but the wicked shall fall into mischief.

C. He Is Protected by Godly Principles

11:6   The righteousness of the upright shall deliver them:
but transgressors shall be taken in their
own naughtiness.

22:5   Thorns and snares are in the way of the froward:
he that doth keep his soul shall be far from them.

16:17   The highway of the upright is to depart from evil:
he that keepeth his way preserveth his soul.

28:18   Whoso walketh uprightly shall be saved:
but he that is perverse in his ways shall fall at once.

10:9   He that walketh uprightly walketh surely:
but he that perverteth his ways shall be known.

19:16   He that keepeth the commandment keepeth
       his own soul;
    but he that despiseth his ways shall die.

  D.   He Is Established by Godly Principles

12:3   A man shall not be established by wickedness:
    but the root of the righteous shall not be moved.

10:30   The righteous shall never be removed:
    but the wicked shall not inhabit the earth.

II. The Believer Has Everlasting Life

10:25   As the whirlwind passeth, so is the wicked no more:
    but the righteous is an everlasting foundation.

14:32   The wicked is driven away in his wickedness:
    but the righteous hath hope in his death.

12:28   In the way of righteousness is life;
    and in the pathway thereof there is no death.

15:24   The way of life is above to the wise,
    that he may depart from hell beneath.

III. The Believer Shares His Spiritual Life With Others

11:30   The fruit of the righteous is a tree of life;
    and he that winneth souls is wise.

10:21   The lips of the righteous feed many:
    but fools die for want of wisdom.

10:11   The mouth of a righteous man is a well of life:
    but violence covereth the mouth of the wicked.

29:10   The bloodthirsty hate the upright:
    but the just seek his soul.

22:19   That thy trust may be in the Lord,
    I have made known to thee this day, even to thee.

    20   Have not I written to thee excellent things
    in counsels and knowledge,

    21   That I might make thee know the certainty
       of the words of truth;
    that thou mightest answer the words of truth
       to them that send unto thee?

THE BELIEVER'S BLESSINGS

I. God Blesses the Believer Inwardly

A.   With Joy and Happiness

16:20   He that handleth a matter wisely shall find good:
and whoso trusteth in the Lord, happy is he.

13:9   The light of the righteous rejoiceth:
but the lamp of the wicked shall be put out.

10:28   The hope of the righteous shall be gladness:
but the expectation of the wicked shall perish.

29:6   In the transgression of an evil man there is a snare:
but the righteous doth sing and rejoice.

B.   With Abundant, Spiritual Life

21:21   He that followeth after righteousness and mercy
findeth life, righteousness, and honour.

II. God Blesses the Believer Outwardly

A.   With Success and Prosperity

10:22   The blessing of the Lord, it maketh rich,
and he addeth no sorrow with it.

28:25   He that is of a proud heart stirreth up strife:
but he that putteth his trust in the Lord
shall be made fat.

28:10   Whoso causeth the righteous to go astray
in an evil way,
he shall fall himself into his own pit:
but the upright shall have good things in possession.

12:12   The wicked desireth the net of evil men:
but the root of the righteous yieldeth fruit.

B.   With Satisfaction of Physical Needs

13:25   The righteous eateth to the satisfying of his soul:
but the belly of the wicked shall want.

10:3   The Lord will not suffer the soul of the righteous
to famish:
but he casteth away the substance of the wicked.

C. With Honor Among Men

11:27   He that diligently seeketh good procureth favour:
         but he that seeketh mischief, it shall come unto him.

14:19   The evil bow before the good;
         and the wicked at the gates of the righteous.

10:7   The memory of the just is blessed:
         but the name of the wicked shall rot.

III. God Blesses the Believer's Home and Family

3:33   The curse of the Lord is in the house of the wicked:
         but he blesseth the habitation of the just.

14:11   The house of the wicked shall be overthrown:
         but the tabernacle of the upright shall flourish.

15:6   In the house of the righteous is much treasure:
         but in the revenues of the wicked is trouble.

20:7   The just man walketh in his integrity:
         his children are blessed after him.

IV. God Blesses the Believer Completely and Continually

12:2   A good man obtaineth favour of the Lord:
         but a man of wicked devices will he condemn.

11:31   Behold, the righteous shall be recompensed
              in the earth:
         much more the wicked and the sinner.

13:21   Evil pursueth sinners:
         but to the righteous good shall be repayed.

10:6   Blessings are upon the head of the just:
         but violence covereth the mouth of the wicked.

10:24   The fear of the wicked, it shall come upon him:
         but the desire of the righteous shall be granted.

THE BELIEVER'S PROTECTION

I. **God Protects the Believer**

A. From Trouble and Adversity

11:8 The righteous is delivered out of trouble,
and the wicked cometh in his stead.

12:13 The wicked is snared by the transgression of his lips:
but the just shall come out of trouble.

12:21 There shall no evil happen to the just:
but the wicked shall be filled with mischief.

B. From Danger and Injury

18:10 The name of the Lord is a strong tower:
the righteous runneth into it, and is safe.

22:31 The horse is prepared against the day of battle:
but safety is of the Lord.

30:5 Every word of God is pure:
he is a shield unto them that put their trust in him.

2:7 He layeth up sound wisdom for the righteous:
he is a buckler to them that walk uprightly.

8 He keepeth the paths of judgment,
and preserveth the way of his saints.

C. From Fear and Distress

29:25 The fear of man bringeth a snare:
but whoso putteth his trust in the Lord
shall be safe.

3:24 When thou liest down, thou shalt not be afraid:
yea, thou shalt lie down, and thy sleep
shall be sweet.

25 Be not afraid of sudden fear,
neither of the desolation of the wicked,
when it cometh.

26 For the Lord shall be thy confidence,
and shall keep thy foot from being taken.

20:22 Say not thou, I will recompense evil;
but wait on the Lord, and he shall save thee.

II. **God Protects the Believer's Descendants**

14:26   In the fear of the Lord is strong confidence:
  and his children shall have a place of refuge.

11:21   Though hand join in hand,
  the wicked shall not be unpunished:
  but the seed of the righteous shall be delivered.

III. **God Protects the Believer's Home**

12:7   The wicked are overthrown, and are not:
  but the house of the righteous shall stand.

24:15   Lay not wait, O wicked man,
  against the dwelling of the righteous;
  spoil not his resting place:
 16   For a just man falleth seven times,
   and riseth up again:
  but the wicked shall fall into mischief.

Chapter 5

Invaluable Wisdom

When wisdom entereth into thine heart,
and knowledge is pleasant unto thy soul;
Discretion shall preserve thee,
understanding shall keep thee.

(2:10-11)

Page

The Nature of Wisdom 50

The Benefits of Wisdom................................ 53

Comparisons and Contrasts to Wisdom 56

The Constant Call of Wisdom 57

THE NATURE OF WISDOM

I. **Wisdom Is From the Lord**

A. It Stems From a Personal Relationship With God

9:10 The fear of the Lord is the beginning of wisdom:
and the knowledge of the Holy is understanding.

15:33 The fear of the Lord is the instruction of wisdom;
and before honour is humility.

28:5 Evil men understand not judgment:
but they that seek the Lord understand all things.

B. God Gives It Increasingly to Those Who Walk With Him

2:6 For the Lord giveth wisdom:
out of his mouth cometh knowledge
and understanding.

7 He layeth up sound wisdom for the righteous:
he is a buckler to them that walk uprightly.

8 He keepeth the paths of judgment,
and preserveth the way of his saints.

9 Then shalt thou understand righteousness,
and judgment, and equity;
yea, every good path.

II. **Wisdom and Righteousness Are Inseparable**

A. Righteousness Is a Basic Ingredient of Wisdom

8:6 Hear; for I will speak of excellent things;
and the opening of my lips shall be right things.

7 For my mouth shall speak truth;
and wickedness is an abomination to my lips.

8 All the words of my mouth are in righteousness;
there is nothing froward or perverse in them.

9 They are all plain to him that understandeth,
and right to them that find knowledge.

B. Wisdom Results in a Righteous Life

15:21 Folly is joy to him that is destitute of wisdom:
but a man of understanding walketh uprightly.

8:20 I [wisdom] lead in the way of righteousness,
       in the midst of the paths of judgment:

14:16 A wise man feareth, and departeth from evil:
        but the fool rageth, and is confident.

III. **Wisdom Is the Key to Successful Living** (1:1-7)

A. For Understanding Principles of Right Behavior

1:1 The proverbs of Solomon the son of David,
         king of Israel;
  2 To know wisdom and instruction;
        to perceive the words of understanding;
  3 To receive the instruction of wisdom,
        [practicing] justice, and judgment, and equity;

B. For Insight and Discernment in Making Decisions

1:4 To give subtilty to the simple,
        to the young man knowledge and discretion.
  5 A wise man will hear, and will increase learning;
        and a man of understanding shall attain unto
             wise counsels:
  6 To understand a proverb, and the interpretation;
        the words of the wise, and their dark sayings.

C. For Proper Use of Knowledge

1:7 The fear of the Lord is the beginning of knowledge:
        but fools despise wisdom and instruction.

IV. **Wisdom Characterizes Those Who Possess It**

A. It Is Basic to Their Nature and Character

16:21 The wise in heart shall be called prudent:
          and the sweetness of the lips increaseth learning.
   22 Understanding is a wellspring of life
          unto him that hath it:
          but the instruction of fools is folly.

14:33 Wisdom resteth in the heart of him that hath
           understanding:
         but that which is in the midst of fools
           is made known.

17:24   Wisdom is before him that hath understanding;
　　　　　but the eyes of a fool are in the ends of the earth.

B.   It Is Evident in Their Life and Speech

10:13   In the lips of him that hath understanding
　　　　　　　wisdom is found:
　　　　　but a rod is for the back of him that is void
　　　　　　　of understanding.

　　14   Wise men lay up knowledge:
　　　　　but the mouth of the foolish is near destruction.

10:23   It is as sport to a fool to do mischief:
　　　　　but a man of understanding hath wisdom.

V. Human Wisdom Is Not to Be Trusted

A.   It Cannot Give Proper Direction to Life

3:5   Trust in the Lord with all thine heart;
　　　　and lean not unto thine own understanding.

6   In all thy ways acknowledge him,
　　　and he shall direct thy paths.

7   Be not wise in thine own eyes:
　　　fear the Lord, and depart from evil.

20:24   Man's goings are of the Lord;
　　　　　how can a man then understand his own way?

B.   It Leads to Foolish Attitudes and Actions

28:26   He that trusteth in his own heart is a fool:
　　　　　but whoso walketh wisely, he shall be delivered.

19:3   The foolishness of man perverteth his way:
　　　　　and his heart fretteth against the Lord.

21:8   The way of man is froward and strange:
　　　　　but as for the pure, his work is right.

C.   It Eventually Leads to Death

16:25   There is a way that seemeth right unto a man,
　　　　　but the end thereof are the ways of death.

THE BENEFITS OF WISDOM

I. **Wisdom Contributes to a Full, Rewarding Life**

A. Abundant Spiritual Life and Blessing

3:21 My son, let not them depart from thine eyes:
keep sound wisdom and discretion:
22 So shall they be life unto thy soul,
and grace to thy neck.

19:8 He that getteth wisdom loveth his own soul:
he that keepeth understanding shall find good.

B. Happiness and Satisfaction

3:13 Happy is the man that findeth wisdom,
and the man that getteth understanding.

3:17 Her ways are ways of pleasantness,
and all her paths are peace.
18 She is a tree of life to them that lay hold upon her:
and happy is every one that retaineth her.

24:13 My son, eat thou honey, because it is good;
and the honeycomb, which is sweet to thy taste:
14 So shall the knowledge of wisdom be unto thy soul:
when thou hast found it, then there shall be
a reward,
and thy expectation shall not be cut off.

C. Competence and Inner Strength

14:8 The wisdom of the prudent is to understand his way:
but the folly of fools is deceit.

24:5 A wise man is strong;
yea, a man of knowledge increaseth strength.

21:22 A wise man scaleth the city of the mighty,
and casteth down the strength of the
confidence thereof.

D. Honor and Respect

3:35 The wise shall inherit glory:
but shame shall be the promotion of fools.

12:8   A man shall be commended according to his wisdom:
   but he that is of a perverse heart
    shall be despised.

4:8   Exalt her, and she shall promote thee:
   she shall bring thee to honour,
    when thou dost embrace her.

9   She shall give to thine head an ornament of grace:
   a crown of glory shall she deliver to thee.

13:15   Good understanding giveth favour:
   but the way of transgressors is hard.

E.   Prosperity and Long Life

3:16   Length of days is in her right hand;
   and in her left hand riches and honour.

8:21   That I may cause those that love me
   to inherit substance;
   and I will fill their treasures.

F.   A Successful Home

24:3   Through wisdom is an house builded;
   and by understanding it is established:

4   And by knowledge shall the chambers be filled
   with all precious and pleasant riches.

14:1   Every wise woman buildeth her house:
   but the foolish plucketh it down with her hands.

II. Wisdom Provides Protection

A.   From Harmful Situations

4:6   Forsake her not, and she shall preserve thee:
   love her, and she shall keep thee.

1:33   But whoso hearkeneth unto me shall dwell safely,
   and shall be quiet from fear of evil.

B.   From Making Serious Mistakes

3:21   My son, let not them depart from thine eyes:
   keep sound wisdom and discretion: . . .

23   Then shalt thou walk in thy way safely,
   and thy foot shall not stumble.

4:11　I have taught thee in the way of wisdom;
　　　　I have led thee in right paths.
　12　When thou goest, thy steps shall not be straitened;
　　　　and when thou runnest, thou shalt not stumble.

C.　From Evil People and Evil Deeds

2:10　When wisdom entereth into thine heart,
　　　　and knowledge is pleasant unto thy soul;
　11　Discretion shall preserve thee,
　　　　understanding shall keep thee:
　12　To deliver thee from the way of the evil man,
　　　　from the man that speaketh froward things;
　13　Who leave the paths of uprightness,
　　　　to walk in the ways of darkness; . . .
　16　To deliver thee from the strange woman,
　　　　even from the stranger which flattereth with
　　　　　　her words;
　17　Which forsaketh the guide [partner] of her youth,
　　　　and forgetteth the covenant of her God.

7:4　Say unto wisdom, Thou art my sister;
　　　　and call understanding thy kinswoman:
　5　That they may keep thee from the strange woman,
　　　　from the stranger which flattereth with her words.

III. **Wisdom Is of Paramount Value**

16:16　How much better is it to get wisdom than gold!
　　　　and to get understanding rather to be chosen
　　　　　　than silver!

3:14　For the merchandise of it is better than the
　　　　　　merchandise of silver,
　　　　and the gain thereof than fine gold.
　15　She is more precious than rubies:
　　　　and all the things thou canst desire
　　　　　　are not to be compared unto her.

4:7　Wisdom is the principal thing; therefore get wisdom:
　　　　and with all thy getting get understanding.

COMPARISONS AND CONTRASTS TO WISDOM (Chapter 9)

I. **God's Wisdom (Personified as a Woman)**

 A. Wisdom Is Constructive and Productive

  9:1 Wisdom hath builded her house,
    she hath hewn out her seven pillars:

   2 She hath killed her beasts;
    she hath mingled her wine;
    she hath also furnished her table.

 B. Wisdom Invites the Naive to Learn Her Wholesome Ways

  9:3 She hath sent forth her maidens:
    she crieth upon the highest places of the city,

   4 Whoso is simple, let him turn in hither:
    as for him that wanteth understanding, she saith
     to him,

   5 Come, eat of my bread, and drink of the wine
    which I have mingled.

 C. Wisdom Offers True and Meaningful Life

  9:6 Forsake the foolish, and live;
    and go in the way of understanding.

II. *Obtaining Wisdom*

 A. Wisdom Cannot Be Forced on the Unwilling

  9:7 He that reproveth a scorner getteth to himself shame:
    and he that rebuketh a wicked man getteth himself
     a blot.

   8 Reprove not a scorner, lest he hate thee:
    rebuke a wise man, and he will love thee.

   9 Give instruction to a wise man,
    and he will be yet wiser:
    teach a just man, and he will increase in learning.

 B. Wisdom Must Begin With the Fear of the Lord

  9:10 The fear of the Lord is the beginning of wisdom:
    and the knowledge of the Holy is understanding.

   11 For by me thy days shall be multiplied,
    and the years of thy life shall be increased.

C.   Each Person Must Choose Wisdom for Himself

9:12   If thou be wise, thou shalt be wise for thyself:
    but if thou scornest, thou alone shalt bear it.

III. **Self-Gratifying Foolishness (Personified as a Woman)**

A.   Foolishness Is Undiscerning and Unproductive

9:13   A foolish woman is clamorous:
    she is simple, and knoweth nothing.
14   For she sitteth at the door of her house,
    on a seat in the high places of the city,

B.   Foolishness Entices the Naive With Illicit Pleasure

9:15   To call passengers who go right on their ways:
16   Whoso is simple, let him turn in hither:
    and as for him that wanteth understanding,
        she saith to him,
17   Stolen waters are sweet,
    and bread eaten in secret is pleasant.

C.   Foolishness Deceives and Destroys Her Followers

9:18   But he knoweth not that the dead are there;
    and that her guests are in the depths of hell.

THE CONSTANT CALL OF WISDOM

I. **God's Wisdom Continually Calls to Us** (Chapter 8)

A.   Wisdom Is Offered to Everyone . . .

1.   To All Who Will Listen

8:1   Doth not wisdom cry?
    and understanding put forth her voice?
2   She standeth in the top of high places,
    by the way in the places of the paths.
3   She crieth at the gates, at the entry of the city,
    at the coming in at the doors.

2.   To the Younger and the Older

8:4   Unto you, O men, I call;
    and my voice is to the sons of man.

3. To the Unknowing and the "All-Knowing"

8:5   O ye simple, understand wisdom:
  and, ye fools, be ye of an understanding heart.

B. But Only in Combination With Righteousness

8:6   Hear; for I will speak of excellent things;
  and the opening of my lips shall be right things.
7   For my mouth shall speak truth;
  and wickedness is an abomination to my lips.
8   All the words of my mouth are in righteousness;
  there is nothing froward or perverse in them.
9   They are all plain to him that understandeth,
  and right to them that find knowledge.

C. Nothing Is More Valuable Than Wisdom

1. Wisdom Is Precious

8:10   Receive my instruction, and not silver;
  and knowledge rather than choice gold.
11   For wisdom is better than rubies;
  and all the things that may be desired
   are not to be compared to it.

2. Wisdom Is Practical and Productive

8:12   I wisdom dwell with prudence,
  and find out knowledge of witty inventions.

3. Wisdom Is Pure

8:13   The fear of the Lord is to hate evil:
  pride, and arrogancy, and the evil way,
   and the froward mouth, do I hate.

4. Wisdom Is Powerful

8:14   Counsel is mine, and sound wisdom:
  I am understanding; I have strength.
15   By me kings reign,
  and princes decree justice.
16   By me princes rule, and nobles,
  even all the judges of the earth.

D. Those Who Truly Want Wisdom May Have It

8:17   I love them that love me;
  and those that seek me early shall find me.

18 Riches and honour are with me;
  yea, durable riches and righteousness.
19 My fruit is better than gold, yea, than fine gold;
  and my revenue than choice silver.
20 I lead in the way of righteousness,
  in the midst of the paths of judgment:
21 That I may cause those that love me
    to inherit substance;
  and I will fill their treasures.

E. Christ Reveals God's Wisdom to Men

1. He Is the "I Am" (From Everlasting to Everlasting)

8:22 The Lord possessed me in the beginning of his way,
  before his works of old.
23 I was set up from everlasting,
  from the beginning, or ever the earth was.
24 When there were no depths, I was brought forth;
  when there were no fountains abounding
    with water.
25 Before the mountains were settled,
  before the hills was I brought forth:
26 While as yet he had not made the earth,
    nor the fields,
  nor the highest part of the dust of the world.

2. He Is Elohim (The Triune God of Creation)

8:27 When he prepared the heavens, I was there:
  when he set a compass upon the face of the depth:
28 When he established the clouds above:
  when he strengthened the fountains of the deep:
29 When he gave to the sea his decree,
  that the waters should not pass his commandment:
  when he appointed the foundations of the earth:

3. He Is Emmanuel (God With Us)

8:30 Then I was by him, as one brought up with him:
  and I was daily his delight,
    rejoicing always before him;
31 Rejoicing in the habitable part of his earth;
  and my delights were with the sons of men.

F. Your Response Determines Your Life and Your Eternity

8:32   Now therefore hearken unto me, O ye children:
       for blessed are they that keep my ways.
33   Hear instruction, and be wise, and refuse it not.
34   Blessed is the man that heareth me,
       watching daily at my gates,
       waiting at the posts of my doors.
35   For whoso findeth me findeth life,
       and shall obtain favour of the Lord.
36   But he that sinneth against me wrongeth
       his own soul:
       all they that hate me love death.

II. Wisdom Calls Again and Again (From Chapter 1)

A. Wisdom Is Offered to Everyone

1:20   Wisdom crieth without;
       she uttereth her voice in the streets:
21   She crieth in the chief place of concourse,
       in the openings of the gates:
       in the city she uttereth her words, saying,
22   How long, ye simple ones, will ye love simplicity?
       and the scorners delight in their scorning,
       and fools hate knowledge?
23   Turn you at my reproof:
       behold, I will pour out my spirit unto you,
       I will make known my words unto you.

B. Your Response Determines Your Life and Your Eternity

1:24   Because I have called, and ye refused;
       I have stretched out my hand,
       and no man regarded; . . .
29   For that they hated knowledge,
       and did not choose the fear of the Lord: . . .
31   Therefore shall they eat of the fruit
       of their own way,
       and be filled with their own devices.
32   For the turning away of the simple shall slay them,
       and the prosperity of fools shall destroy them.
33   But whoso hearkeneth unto me shall dwell safely,
       and shall be quiet from fear of evil.

Chapter 6

Knowledge and Instruction — Building Blocks for Life

*Apply thine heart unto instruction,
and thine ears to the words of knowledge.*

(23:12)

Page

Learning and Knowledge 62

Instruction and Counsel 65

Reproof and Correction 67

LEARNING AND KNOWLEDGE

I. Knowledge Is Awareness of Part of God's Truth

A. All Knowledge Derives From and Depends Upon God

2:6   For the Lord giveth wisdom:
out of his mouth cometh knowledge
and understanding.

22:12   The eyes of the Lord preserve knowledge,
and he overthroweth the words of the transgressor.

B. Much Knowledge Is Best Understood by Believers

1:7   The fear of the Lord is the beginning of knowledge:
but fools despise wisdom and instruction.

14:6   A scorner seeketh wisdom, and findeth it not:
but knowledge is easy unto him that understandeth.

8:8   All the words of my mouth are in righteousness;
there is nothing froward or perverse in them.

9   They are all plain to him that understandeth,
and right to them that find knowledge.

C. Spiritual Knowledge Strengthens Faith and Godly Living

22:20   Have not I written to thee excellent things
in counsels and knowledge,

21   That I might make thee know the certainty of the
words of truth;
that thou mightest answer the words of truth
to them that send unto thee?

9:10   The fear of the Lord is the beginning of wisdom:
and the knowledge of the holy is understanding.

19:2   Also, that the soul be without knowledge,
it is not good;
and he that hasteth with his feet sinneth.

II. Knowledge Is Beneficial and Valuable

A. For Competence and Authority

24:5   A wise man is strong;
yea, a man of knowledge increaseth strength.

28:2   For the transgression of a land many are the
         princes thereof:
         but by a man of understanding and knowledge
           the state thereof shall be prolonged.

B.   For Satisfaction and Enjoyment

20:15   There is gold, and a multitude of rubies:
         but the lips of knowledge are a precious jewel.

24:4   And by knowledge shall the chambers be filled
         with all precious and pleasant riches.

22:17   Bow down thine ear, and hear the words of the wise,
         and apply thine heart unto my knowledge.
   18   For it is a pleasant thing if thou keep them
         within thee;
         they shall withal be fitted in thy lips.

C.   For Protection and Security

2:10   When wisdom entereth into thine heart,
         and knowledge is pleasant unto thy soul;
   11   Discretion shall preserve thee,
         understanding shall keep thee:

11:9   An hypocrite with his mouth destroyeth
         his neighbour:
         but through knowledge shall the just be delivered.

III. The Wise Person Continually Increases His Knowledge

A.   He Is Eager to Learn

18:15   The heart of the prudent getteth knowledge;
         and the ear of the wise seeketh knowledge.

15:14   The heart of him that hath understanding
         seeketh knowledge:
         but the mouth of fools feedeth on foolishness.

10:14   Wise men lay up knowledge:
         but the mouth of the foolish is near destruction.

21:11   When the scorner is punished, the simple is
         made wise:
         and when the wise is instructed, he receiveth
         knowledge.

B. He Puts His Knowledge to Good Use

13:16   Every prudent man dealeth with knowledge:
　　　　　but a fool layeth open his folly.

15:2   The tongue of the wise useth knowledge aright:
　　　　　but the mouth of fools poureth out foolishness.

15:7   The lips of the wise disperse knowledge:
　　　　　but the heart of the foolish doeth not so.

IV. **Only Fools Reject Valuable Knowledge**

1:22   How long, ye simple ones, will ye love simplicity?
　　　　　and the scorners delight in their scorning,
　　　　　and fools hate knowledge? . . .

28   Then shall they call upon me, but I will not answer;
　　　　　they shall seek me early, but they shall not find me:

29   For that they hated knowledge,
　　　　　and did not choose the fear of the Lord:

V. **Determine to Obtain Valuable Knowledge**

A. Work Diligently for It

23:12   Apply thine heart unto instruction,
　　　　　and thine ears to the words of knowledge.

25:2   It is the glory of God to conceal a thing:
　　　　　but the honour of kings is to search out a matter.

B. Expect That Your Efforts Will Be Rewarded

2:3   Yea, if thou criest after knowledge,
　　　　　and liftest up thy voice of understanding;

4   If thou seekest her as silver,
　　　　　and searchest for her as for hid treasures;

5   Then shalt thou understand the fear of the Lord,
　　　　　and find the knowledge of God.

6   For the Lord giveth wisdom:
　　　　　out of his mouth cometh knowledge
　　　　　　and understanding.

14:18   The simple inherit folly:
　　　　　but the prudent are crowned with knowledge.

INSTRUCTION AND COUNSEL

I. **Seek and Follow Good Instruction**

   A.   Recognize the Value of Good Instruction

   23:23   Buy the truth, and sell it not;
   also wisdom, and instruction, and understanding.

   10:17   He is in the way of life that keepeth instruction:
   but he that refuseth reproof erreth.

   4:13   Take fast hold of instruction; let her not go:
   keep her; for she is thy life.

   8:10   Receive my instruction, and not silver;
   and knowledge rather than choice gold.

   B.   Be Teachable

   9:9   Give instruction to a wise man, and he will be
   yet wiser:
   teach a just man, and he will increase in learning.

   10:8   The wise in heart will receive commandments:
   but a prating [babbling] fool shall fall.

   12:1   Whoso loveth instruction loveth knowledge:
   but he that hateth reproof is brutish.

   8:33   Hear instruction, and be wise,
   and refuse it not.

   C.   Receive Instruction From Godly Parents

   1:8   My son, hear the instruction of thy father,
   and forsake not the law of thy mother:

   9   For they shall be an ornament of grace
   unto thy head,
   and chains about thy neck.

   4:1   Hear, ye children, the instruction of a father,
   and attend to know understanding.

   2   For I give you good doctrine,
   forsake ye not my law.

   3   For I was my father's son,
   tender and only beloved in the sight of my mother.

4   He taught me also, and said unto me,
Let thine heart retain my words:
keep my commandments, and live.

13:1   A wise son heareth his father's instruction:
but a scorner heareth not rebuke.

D. Do Not Refuse Good Instruction

13:18   Poverty and shame shall be to him that refuseth
instruction:
but he that regardeth reproof shall be honoured.

15:32   He that refuseth instruction despiseth his own soul:
but he that heareth reproof getteth understanding.

5:11   And thou mourn at the last,
when thy flesh and thy body are consumed,

12   And say, How have I hated instruction,
and my heart despised reproof;

13   And have not obeyed the voice of my teachers,
nor inclined mine ear to them that instructed me!

II. **Obtain Good Counsel for Important Decisions**

A. It Improves Your Likelihood of Success

20:18   Every purpose is established by counsel:
and with good advice make war.

15:22   Without counsel purposes are disappointed:
but in the multitude of counsellors
they are established.

B. It Increases Your Wisdom

19:20   Hear counsel, and receive instruction,
that thou mayest be wise in thy latter end.

12:15   The way of a fool is right in his own eyes:
but he that hearkeneth unto counsel is wise.

13:10   Only by pride cometh contention:
but with the well advised is wisdom.

III. **Be Careful and Selective in Obtaining Counsel**

A.   Seek Out Wise Counselors

1:5   A wise man will hear, and will increase learning;
and a man of understanding shall attain unto
wise counsels:

B.   Obtain Counsel From Several Sources

11:14   Where no counsel is, the people fall:
but in the multitude of counsellors there is safety.

24:6   For by wise counsel thou shalt make thy war:
and in multitude of counsellors there is safety.

C.   Seek Thorough, Candid Counsel

20:5   Counsel in the heart of man is like deep water;
but a man of understanding will draw it out.

D.   Value Counsel From a Close Friend

27:9   Ointment and perfume rejoice the heart:
so doth the sweetness of a man's friend
by hearty counsel.

E.   Disregard Ungodly Counsel

19:27   Cease, my son, to hear the instruction
that causeth to err from the words of knowledge.

12:5   The thoughts of the righteous are right:
but the counsels of the wicked are deceit.

REPROOF AND CORRECTION

I. **God Chastens and Corrects Those He Loves**

3:11   My son, despise not the chastening of the Lord;
neither be weary of his correction:

12   For whom the Lord loveth he correcteth;
even as a father the son in whom he delighteth.

II. **A Wise Person Accepts and Benefits From Correction**

A.   Correction Increases Wisdom and Knowledge

15:31   The ear that heareth the reproof of life
　　　　abideth among the wise.

32   He that refuseth instruction despiseth his own soul:
　　　 but he that heareth reproof getteth understanding.

15:5   A fool despiseth his father's instruction:
　　　 but he that regardeth reproof is prudent.

1:20   Wisdom crieth without;
　　　 she uttereth her voice in the streets: . . .

23   Turn you at my reproof:
　　　 behold, I will pour out my spirit unto you,
　　　 I will make known my words unto you.

19:25   Smite a scorner, and the simple will beware:
　　　　 and reprove one that hath understanding,
　　　　　 and he will understand knowledge.

B.   Heeded Correction Brings Honor

13:18   Poverty and shame shall be to him that refuseth
　　　　　 instruction:
　　　　 but he that regardeth reproof shall be honoured.

C.   Refusal of Correction Brings Destruction

29:1   He, that being often reproved hardeneth his neck,
　　　 shall suddenly be destroyed, and that
　　　　 without remedy.

15:10   Correction is grievous unto him
　　　　 that forsaketh the way:
　　　 and he that hateth reproof shall die.

1:30   They would none of my counsel:
　　　 they despised all my reproof.

31   Therefore shall they eat of the fruit
　　　 of their own way,
　　 and be filled with their own devices.

32   For the turning away of the simple shall slay them,
　　 and the prosperity of fools shall destroy them.

III. **Oral Correction Should Be Sufficient for a Wise Person**

17:10 A reproof entereth more into a wise man
        than an hundred stripes into a fool.

IV. **Physical Punishment Is Necessary and Beneficial at Times**

A. It Helps Teach Erring Children to Live Uprightly

22:15 Foolishness is bound in the heart of a child;
        but the rod of correction shall drive it far from him.

23:13 Withhold not correction from the child:
        for if thou beatest him with the rod,
          he shall not die.
   14 Thou shalt beat him with the rod,
        and shalt deliver his soul from hell.

19:18 Chasten thy son while there is hope,
        and let not thy soul spare for his crying.

29:15 The rod and reproof give wisdom:
        but a child left to himself bringeth his mother
          to shame.

13:24 He that spareth his rod hateth his son:
        but he that loveth him chasteneth him betimes.

29:17 Correct thy son, and he shall give thee rest;
        yea, he shall give delight unto thy soul.

B. It Helps Cleanse a Guilty Conscience

20:30 The blueness of a wound cleanseth away evil:
        so do stripes the inward parts of the belly.

C. It Helps Teach Those Who Otherwise Do Not Learn

10:13 In the lips of him that hath understanding
          wisdom is found:
        but a rod is for the back of him that is void of
          understanding.

D. It Is a Proper Reward for Foolish Behavior

19:29 Judgments are prepared for scorners,
        and stripes for the back of fools.

26:3 A whip for the horse, a bridle for the ass,
        and a rod for the fool's back.

E. It Warns Naive Observers of the Consequences of
Wrong-Doing

21:11   When the scorner is punished, the simple
is made wise:
and when the wise is instructed, he receiveth
knowledge.

19:25   Smite a scorner, and the simple will beware:
and reprove one that hath understanding,
and he will understand knowledge.

V. Correcting Others Requires Skill and Discretion

A. A Scoffer Won't Accept Correction; A Wise Person Will

9:7   He that reproveth a scorner getteth to himself shame:
and he that rebuketh a wicked man getteth
himself a blot.

8   Reprove not a scorner, lest he hate thee:
rebuke a wise man, and he will love thee.

B. Normally, It Is Unwise to Correct a Fool

26:4   Answer not a fool according to his folly,
lest thou also be like unto him.

C. At Times, However, a Fool Must Be Set Straight

26:5   Answer a fool according to his folly,
lest he be wise in his own conceit.

D. Verbal Correction May Be Insufficient for Some

29:19   A servant will not be corrected by words:
for though he understand he will not answer.

VI. Proper Correction Builds and Strengthens Relationships

28:23   He that rebuketh a man afterwards shall
find more favour
than he that flattereth with the tongue.

27:5   Open rebuke is better than secret love.

6   Faithful are the wounds of a friend;
but the kisses of an enemy are deceitful.

25:12   As an earring of gold, and an ornament of fine gold,
so is a wise reprover upon an obedient ear.

Chapter 7

The Disciplined Heart and Mind

Keep thy heart with all diligence;
for out of it are the issues of life. . . .
Ponder the path of thy feet,
and let all thy ways be established.

(4:23, 26)

	Page
Thoughts	72
Pride	74
Humility	76
Prudence and Caution	78

THOUGHTS

I. **Your Thoughts Govern Your Life**

  A. They Tell What You Really Are Inside

12:5   The thoughts of the righteous are right:
          but the counsels of the wicked are deceit.

23:7   For as he thinketh in his heart, so is he:
          eat and drink, saith he to thee;
          but his heart is not with thee.

12:20   Deceit is in the heart of them that imagine evil:
          but to the counsellors of peace is joy.

27:19   As in water face answereth to face,
          so the heart of man to man.

  B. They Determine the Direction and Outcome of Your Life

4:23   Keep thy heart with all diligence;
          for out of it are the issues of life. . . .

26   Ponder the path of thy feet,
          and let all thy ways be established.

21:5   The thoughts of the diligent tend only
          to plenteousness;
          but of every one that is hasty only to want.

14:22   Do they not err that devise evil?
          but mercy and truth shall be to them that
          devise good.

II. **God Cares About Your Thoughts**

  A. He Knows All of Your Thoughts

15:11   Hell and destruction are before the Lord:
          how much more then the hearts of the
          children of men?

21:2   Every way of a man is right in his own eyes:
          but the Lord pondereth the hearts.

20:27   The spirit of man is the candle of the Lord,
          searching all the inward parts of the belly.

B. He Hates Evil Thoughts

6:16   These six things doth the Lord hate:
   yea, seven are an abomination unto him: . . .
18   An heart that deviseth wicked imaginations,
   feet that be swift in running to mischief,

15:26   The thoughts of the wicked are an abomination
   to the Lord:
   but the words of the pure are pleasant words.

24:8   He that deviseth to do evil
   shall be called a mischievous person.
9   The thought of foolishness is sin:
   and the scorner is an abomination to men.

C. He Overrules Thoughts Contrary to His Will

19:21   There are many devices in a man's heart;
   nevertheless the counsel of the Lord,
    that shall stand.

16:9   A man's heart deviseth his way:
   but the Lord directeth his steps.

22:30   There is no wisdom nor understanding
   nor counsel against the Lord.

D. He Rewards and Fulfills Righteous Thoughts

14:22   Do they not err that devise evil?
   but mercy and truth shall be to them
    that devise good.

10:24   The fear of the wicked, it shall come upon him:
   but the desire of the righteous shall be granted.

III. **Let God Direct Your Thoughts**

A. Put Away Improper Thoughts

30:32   If thou hast done foolishly in lifting up thyself,
   or if thou hast thought evil,
   lay thine hand upon thy mouth.

B. Submit Your Thought-Life to God

16:1   The preparations of the heart in man,
   and the answer of the tongue, is from the Lord.

2   All the ways of a man are clean in his own eyes;
        but the Lord weigheth the spirits.

3   Commit thy works unto the Lord,
        and thy thoughts shall be established.

PRIDE

I. Pride Is Sin

21:4   An high look, and a proud heart,
            and the plowing of the wicked, is sin.

II. Pride Incurs God's Wrath

16:5   Every one that is proud in heart
                is an abomination to the Lord:
            though hand join in hand,
                he shall not be unpunished.

6:16   These six things doth the Lord hate:
            yea, seven are an abomination unto him:

17   A proud look, a lying tongue,
            and hands that shed innocent blood, . . .

8:13   The fear of the Lord is to hate evil:
            pride, and arrogancy, and the evil way,
                and the froward mouth, do I hate.

III. Pride Produces Harmful Attitudes and Behavior

A.   Turning Away From God

30:8   Remove far from me vanity and lies:
            give me neither poverty nor riches;
            feed me with food convenient for me:

9   Lest I be full, and deny thee,
                and say, Who is the Lord?
            or lest I be poor, and steal,
                and take the name of my God in vain.

B.   Foolish Speech and Foolish Actions

14:3   In the mouth of the foolish is a rod of pride:
            but the lips of the wise shall preserve them.

28:26 He that trusteth in his own heart is a fool:
   but whoso walketh wisely, he shall be delivered.

28:25 He that is of a proud heart stirreth up strife:
   but he that putteth his trust in the Lord
    shall be made fat.

13:10 Only by pride cometh contention:
   but with the well advised is wisdom.

 C. Arrogance and Rebellion

21:24 Proud and haughty scorner is his name,
   who dealeth in proud wrath.

30:11 There is a generation that curseth their father,
   and doth not bless their mother.
  12 There is a generation that are pure in their own eyes,
   and yet is not washed from their filthiness.
  13 There is a generation, O how lofty are their eyes!
   and their eyelids are lifted up.

IV. **Pride Brings Disgrace and Ruin**

 A. Embarrassment and Shame

29:23 A man's pride shall bring him low:
   but honour shall uphold the humble in spirit.

11:2 When pride cometh, then cometh shame:
   but with the lowly is wisdom.

 B. Defeat and Destruction

16:18 Pride goeth before destruction,
   and an haughty spirit before a fall.

18:12 Before destruction the heart of man is haughty,
   and before honour is humility.

26:12 Seest thou a man wise in his own conceit?
   there is more hope of a fool than of him.

17:19 He loveth transgression that loveth strife:
   and he that exalteth his gate seeketh destruction.

15:25 The Lord will destroy the house of the proud:
   but he will establish the border of the widow.

V. **Work, Therefore, to Overcome Pride**

A. Don't Overestimate Yourself

3:7   Be not wise in thine own eyes:
       fear the Lord, and depart from evil.

27:1   Boast not thyself of tomorrow;
       for thou knowest not what a day may bring forth.

B. Don't Praise Yourself

27:2   Let another man praise thee, and not
              thine own mouth;
       a stranger, and not thine own lips.

12:9   He that is despised, and hath a servant,
              is better than he that honoureth himself,
              and lacketh bread.

20:6   Most men will proclaim every one his own goodness:
       but a faithful man who can find?

C. Don't Seek Praise

25:27 It is not good to eat much honey:
       so for men to search their own glory is not glory.

D. Don't Become Proud When Commended

27:21 As the fining pot for silver, and the furnace for gold;
       so is a man to his praise.

E. Repent of Pride and Be Done With It

30:32 If thou hast done foolishly in lifting up thyself,
              or if thou hast thought evil,
       lay thine hand upon thy mouth.

HUMILITY

I. **Humility Is Seeing God and Self as Both Really Are** (30:2-9)

A. God's Wisdom and Power vs. My Ignorance and
   Impotence

30:2   Surely I am more brutish than any man,
       and have not the understanding of a man.

3   I neither learned wisdom,
     nor have the knowledge of the holy.
4   Who hath ascended up into heaven, or descended?
     who hath gathered the wind in his fists?
     who hath bound the waters in a garment?
     who hath established all the ends of the earth:
     what is his name, and what is his son's name,
        if thou canst tell?

B. God's Perfection and Authority vs. My Imperfection and Lowliness

30:5   Every word of God is pure:
     he is a shield unto them that put their trust in him.
6   Add thou not unto his words,
     lest he reprove thee, and thou be found a liar.

C. God's Faithfulness and Provision vs. My Unfaithfulness and Dependence

30:7   Two things have I required of thee;
     deny me them not before I die:
8   Remove far from me vanity and lies:
     give me neither poverty nor riches;
     feed me with food convenient for me:
9   Lest I be full, and deny thee,
     and say, Who is the Lord?
     or lest I be poor, and steal,
     and take the name of my God in vain.

II. Humility Is Part of Fearing the Lord

3:7   Be not wise in thine own eyes:
     fear the Lord, and depart from evil.

III. Humility Is Part of Wisdom

11:2   When pride cometh, then cometh shame:
     but with the lowly is wisdom.

IV. Humility Is More Rewarding Than Pride

16:19   Better it is to be of an humble spirit with the lowly,
     than to divide the spoil with the proud.

25:6   Put not forth thyself in the presence of the king,
       and stand not in the place of great men:
  7   For better it is that it be said unto thee,
       Come up hither;
     than that thou shouldest be put lower
       in the presence of the prince
       whom thine eyes have seen.

V. Humility Leads to Honor

15:33   The fear of the Lord is the instruction of wisdom;
      and before honour is humility.

18:12   Before destruction the heart of man is haughty,
      and before honour is humility.

29:23   A man's pride shall bring him low:
      but honour shall uphold the humble in spirit.

VI. Humility Is Blessed by God

3:34   Surely he scorneth the scorners:
     but he giveth grace unto the lowly.

22:4   By humility and the fear of the Lord
     are riches, and honour, and life.

PRUDENCE AND CAUTION

I. Be Careful About the Course of Your Life

A.   Be Diligent in Following God's Path

4:23   Keep thy heart with all diligence;
     for out of it are the issues of life.
  24   Put away from thee a froward mouth,
     and perverse lips put far from thee.
  25   Let thine eyes look right on,
     and let thine eyelids look straight before thee.
  26   Ponder the path of thy feet,
     and let all thy ways be established.
  27   Turn not to the right hand nor to the left:
     remove thy foot from evil.

B. Be Careful Whom and What You Believe

14:15   The simple believeth every word:
   but the prudent man looketh well to his going.

18:17   He that is first in his own cause seemeth just;
   but his neighbour cometh and searcheth him.

29:5   A man that flattereth his neighbour
   spreadeth a net for his feet.

26:24   He that hateth dissembleth [hides it] with his lips,
   and layeth up deceit within him;
 25   When he speaketh fair, believe him not:
   for there are seven abominations in his heart.

C. Be Sure of What You Are Doing

13:16   Every prudent man dealeth with knowledge:
   but a fool layeth open his folly.

14:8   The wisdom of the prudent is to understand his way:
   but the folly of fools is deceit.

18:15   The heart of the prudent getteth knowledge;
   and the ear of the wise seeketh knowledge.

25:2   It is the glory of God to conceal a thing:
   but the honour of kings is to search out a matter.

D. Anticipate Problems and Avoid Them

22:3   A prudent man foreseeth the evil, and hideth himself:
   but the simple pass on, and are punished.

27:12   A prudent man foreseeth the evil, and hideth himself;
   but the simple pass on, and are punished.

16:17   The highway of the upright is to depart from evil:
   he that keepeth his way preserveth his soul.

22:5   Thorns and snares are in the way of the froward:
   he that doth keep his soul shall be far from them.

E. Consider the Consequences of Others' Mistakes

21:12   The righteous man wisely considereth the house of
   the wicked:
   but God overthroweth the wicked
   for their wickedness.

24:30 I went by the field of the slothful,
and by the vineyard of the man
void of understanding;

31 And, lo, it was all grown over with thorns,
and nettles had covered the face thereof,
and the stone wall thereof was broken down.

32 Then I saw, and considered it well:
I looked upon it, and received instruction.

II. **Be Careful and Deliberate in Word and Deed**

A. Haste Leads to Waste and Transgression

21:5 The thoughts of the diligent tend only
to plenteousness;
but of every one that is hasty only to want.

19:2 Also, that the soul be without knowledge,
it is not good;
and he that hasteth with his feet sinneth.

B. A Quick Temper Causes Foolish Actions

14:17 He that is soon angry dealeth foolishly:
and a man of wicked devices is hated.

12:16 A fool's wrath is presently known:
but a prudent man covereth shame.

14:29 He that is slow to wrath is of great understanding:
but he that is hasty of spirit exalteth folly.

C. Jumping to Conclusions Results in Shame

18:13 He that answereth a matter before he heareth it,
it is folly and shame unto him.

25:8 Go not forth hastily to strive,
lest thou know not what to do in the end thereof,
when thy neighbour hath put thee to shame.

D. Haste in Holy Matters Brings Regret

20:25 It is a snare to the man who devoureth
[dedicates rashly] that which is holy,
and after vows to make inquiry.

Chapter 8

*Temperament and Emotions —
Causes and Effects*

*A merry heart maketh a cheerful countenance:
but by sorrow of the heart the spirit is broken.*

(15:13)

	Page
Happiness and Joy	82
Peace and Satisfaction	85
Sorrow and Grief	87
Anger and Hatred	90

HAPPINESS AND JOY

I. **The Basis of True Happiness and Joy**

    A. Faith in God

      16:20 He that handleth a matter wisely shall find good:
             and whoso trusteth in the Lord, happy is he.

    B. Obedience to God's Word

      29:18 Where there is no vision, the people perish:
             but he that keepeth the law, happy is he.

    C. God-Given Wisdom

      3:13 Happy is the man that findeth wisdom,
          and the man that getteth understanding. . . .
        18 She is a tree of life to them that lay hold upon her:
          and happy is every one that retaineth her.

    D. A Righteous Life

      29:6 In the transgression of an evil man there is a snare:
          but the righteous doth sing and rejoice.

      13:9 The light of the righteous rejoiceth:
          but the lamp of the wicked shall be put out.

      28:14 Happy is the man that feareth alway:
            but he that hardeneth his heart shall fall
            into mischief.

      21:15 It is joy to the just to do judgment:
            but destruction shall be to the workers of iniquity.

    E. Kindness and Service to Others

      14:21 He that despiseth his neighbour sinneth:
            but he that hath mercy on the poor, happy is he.

      12:20 Deceit is in the heart of them that imagine evil:
            but to the counsellors of peace is joy.

    F. The Expectation of Future Blessing

      10:28 The hope of the righteous shall be gladness:
            but the expectation of the wicked shall perish.

      31:25 Strength and honour are her clothing;
           and she shall rejoice in time to come.

II. **Key People That Contribute to One's Happiness**

A. Supportive Friends

27:9   Ointment and perfume rejoice the heart:
        so doth the sweetness of a man's friend
        by hearty counsel.

B. A Loving Spouse

5:18   Let thy fountain be blessed:
        and rejoice with the wife of thy youth.

C. Godly Children

1. Wise Children

15:20 A wise son maketh a glad father:
        but a foolish man despiseth his mother.

23:15 My son, if thine heart be wise,
        my heart shall rejoice, even mine.
   16 Yea, my reins [inmost being] shall rejoice,
        when thy lips speak right things.

27:11 My son, be wise, and make my heart glad,
        that I may answer him that reproacheth me.

29:3   Whoso loveth wisdom rejoiceth his father:
        but he that keepeth company with harlots
        spendeth his substance.

2. Righteous Children

23:24 The father of the righteous shall greatly rejoice:
        and he that begetteth a wise child
        shall have joy of him.
   25 Thy father and thy mother shall be glad,
        and she that bare thee shall rejoice.

3. Properly Disciplined Children

29:17 Correct thy son, and he shall give thee rest;
        yea, he shall give delight unto thy soul.

D. Righteous Leadership

29:2   When the righteous are in authority,
        the people rejoice:
        but when the wicked beareth rule, the people mourn.

28:12   When righteous men do rejoice, there is great glory:
   but when the wicked rise, a man is hidden.

11:10   When it goeth well with the righteous,
    the city rejoiceth:
   and when the wicked perish, there is shouting.

III. Circumstances That Bring Happiness for a Time

 A. Sympathetic Encouragement

  12:25   Heaviness in the heart of man maketh it stoop:
     but a good word maketh it glad.

 B. Another's Cheerfulness

  15:30   The light of the eyes rejoiceth the heart:
     and a good report maketh the bones fat.

 C. Righteous Counsel

  16:13   Righteous lips are the delight of kings;
     and they love him that speaketh right.

 D. An Apt Reply

  15:23   A man hath joy by the answer of his mouth:
     and a word spoken in due season, how good is it!

IV. The Effects of True Happiness and Joy

 A. A Positive Attitude Toward the Circumstances of Life

  15:15   All the days of the afflicted are evil:
     but he that is of a merry heart hath a
      continual feast.

 B. Physical Well-Being

  17:22   A merry heart doeth good like a medicine:
     but a broken spirit drieth the bones.

 C. A Cheerful Appearance

  15:13   A merry heart maketh a cheerful countenance:
     but by sorrow of the heart the spirit is broken.

PEACE AND SATISFACTION

I. **The Source of Peace and Satisfaction**

A. A Proper Relationship With God

19:23   The fear of the Lord tendeth to life:
and he that hath it shall abide satisfied;
he shall not be visited with evil.

B. Obedience to God's Word

3:1   My son, forget not my law;
but let thine heart keep my commandments:

2   For length of days, and long life, and peace,
shall they add to thee.

C. A Righteous Life

14:14   The backslider in heart shall be filled with his
own ways:
and a good man shall be satisfied from himself.

13:25   The righteous eateth to the satisfying of his soul:
but the belly of the wicked shall want.

D. God-Given Wisdom

3:21   My son, let not them depart from thine eyes:
keep sound wisdom and discretion: . . .

24   When thou liest down, thou shalt not be afraid:
yea, thou shalt lie down, and thy sleep
shall be sweet.

25   Be not afraid of sudden fear,
neither of the desolation of the wicked,
when it cometh.

26   For the Lord shall be thy confidence,
and shall keep thy foot from being taken.

3:17   Her ways are ways of pleasantness,
and all her paths are peace.

1:33   But whoso hearkeneth unto me shall dwell safely,
and shall be quiet from fear of evil.

II. **The Physical Benefits of Peace and Satisfaction**

14:30   A sound [tranquil] heart is the life of the flesh:
but envy the rottenness of the bones.

18:14   The spirit of a man will sustain his infirmity;
but a wounded spirit who can bear?

III. **Things That Bring Satisfaction for a Time**

A.   Fulfillment of a Desire

13:19   The desire accomplished is sweet to the soul:
but it is abomination to fools to depart from evil.

13:12   Hope deferred maketh the heart sick:
but when the desire cometh, it is a tree of life.

B.   Appropriate Speech

12:14   A man shall be satisfied with good by the fruit of
his mouth:
and the recompence of a man's hands shall be
rendered unto him.

C.   A Faithful Helper

25:13   As the cold of snow in the time of harvest,
so is a faithful messenger to them that send him:
for he refresheth the soul of his masters.

D.   Good News

25:25   As cold waters to a thirsty soul,
so is good news from a far country.

15:30   The light of the eyes rejoiceth the heart:
and a good report maketh the bones fat.

IV. **Things That Cannot Be Satisfied**

A.   The Desires of a Man Apart From God

27:20   Hell and destruction are never full;
so the eyes of man are never satisfied.

B. Additional Natural Desires

30:15   The horseleach hath two daughters, crying,
        Give, give.
    There are three things that are never satisfied,
    yea, four things say not, It is enough.
16   The grave; and the barren womb;
    the earth that is not filled with water;
    and the fire that saith not, It is enough.

SORROW AND GRIEF

I. Basic Causes of Sorrow and Grief

A. Rejection of God's Word and Will

1:24   Because I have called, and ye refused;
    I have stretched out my hand, and no man regarded;
25   But ye have set at nought all my counsel,
    and would none of my reproof:
26   I also will laugh at your calamity;
    I will mock when your fear cometh;
27   When your fear cometh as desolation,
    and your destruction cometh as a whirlwind;
    when distress and anguish cometh upon you.

B. Rejection of Wise Instruction

5:11   And thou mourn at the last,
    when thy flesh and thy body are consumed,
12   And say, How have I hated instruction,
    and my heart despised reproof;
13   And have not obeyed the voice of my teachers,
    nor inclined mine ear to them that instructed me!

C. The Absence of God's Blessing

10:22   The blessing of the Lord, it maketh rich,
    and he addeth no sorrow with it.

II. Practices That Bring Sorrow and Grief

A. Greed and Dishonesty

15:27   He that is greedy of gain troubleth his own house;
    but he that hateth gifts [bribes] shall live.

B. Mistreatment of Others

11:17   The merciful man doeth good to his own soul:
　　　　but he that is cruel troubleth his own flesh.

11:29   He that troubleth his own house shall inherit
　　　　　　the wind:
　　　　and the fool shall be servant to the wise of heart.

C. Trust of Strangers

11:15   He that is surety for a stranger shall smart for it:
　　　　and he that hateth suretiship is sure.

D. Carelessness

22:3   A prudent man foreseeth the evil, and hideth himself:
　　　　but the simple pass on, and are punished.

E. Drunkenness

23:29   Who hath woe? who hath sorrow?
　　　　who hath contentions? who hath babbling?
　　　　who hath wounds without cause?
　　　　who hath redness of eyes?

30   They that tarry long at the wine;
　　　　they that go to seek mixed wine.

F. Sexual Immorality

6:32   But whoso committeth adultery with a woman
　　　　　　lacketh understanding:
　　　　he that doeth it destroyeth his own soul.

33   A wound and dishonour shall he get;
　　　　and his reproach shall not be wiped away.

5:3   For the lips of a strange woman drop
　　　　　　as an honeycomb,
　　　　and her mouth is smoother than oil:

4   But her end is bitter as wormwood,
　　　　sharp as a twoedged sword.

III. People That Cause Sorrow and Grief

A. Unfaithful Associates

25:19   Confidence in an unfaithful man in time of trouble
　　　　is like a broken tooth, and a foot out of joint.

B. Foolish Children

17:25   A foolish son is a grief to his father,
   and bitterness to her that bare him.

17:21   He that begetteth a fool doeth it to his sorrow:
   and the father of a fool hath no joy.

10:1   The proverbs of Solomon.
   A wise son maketh a glad father:
   but a foolish son is the heaviness of his mother.

C. Gossips

26:22   The words of a talebearer are as wounds,
   and they go down into the innermost parts
    of the belly.

D. Wicked Leaders

29:2   When the righteous are in authority,
   the people rejoice:
   but when the wicked beareth rule,
   the people mourn.

IV. **The Effects of Sorrow and Grief**

A. A Heavy, Inner Burden

14:13   Even in laughter the heart is sorrowful;
   and the end of that mirth is heaviness.

14:10   The heart knoweth his own bitterness;
   and a stranger doth not intermeddle with his joy.

25:20   As he that taketh away a garment in cold weather,
   and as vinegar upon nitre [soda],
   so is he that singeth songs to an heavy heart.

B. Sapped Vitality and Discouragement

15:13   A merry heart maketh a cheerful countenance:
   but by sorrow of the heart the spirit is broken.

17:22   A merry heart doeth good like a medicine:
   but a broken spirit drieth the bones.

12:25   Heaviness in the heart of man maketh it stoop:
   but a good word maketh it glad.

18:14   The spirit of a man will sustain his infirmity;
   but a wounded spirit who can bear?

ANGER AND HATRED

I. Anger and Hatred Lead to Further Sin

A. Sinful Words and Deeds

29:22 An angry man stirreth up strife,
and a furious man aboundeth in transgression.

14:17 He that is soon angry dealeth foolishly:
and a man of wicked devices is hated.

B. Lies and Deception

26:24 He that hateth dissembleth with his lips,
and layeth up deceit within him;

25 When he speaketh fair, believe him not:
for there are seven abominations in his heart.

26 Whose hatred is covered by deceit,
his wickedness shall be shewed before the
whole congregation.

10:18 He that hideth hatred with lying lips,
and he that uttereth a slander, is a fool.

C. Dissension and Conflict

15:18 A wrathful man stirreth up strife:
but he that is slow to anger appeaseth strife.

10:12 Hatred stirreth up strifes:
but love covereth all sins.

D. Cruelty and Oppression

27:4 Wrath is cruel, and anger is outrageous;
but who is able to stand before envy?

II. Repeated Anger Will Be Punished

19:19 A man of great wrath shall suffer punishment:
for if thou deliver him, yet thou must do it again.

III. Guard Against Anger and Hatred

A. Control Your Temper

19:11 The discretion of a man deferreth his anger;
and it is his glory to pass over a transgression.

14:29 He that is slow to wrath is of great understanding:
      but he that is hasty of spirit exalteth folly.

16:32 He that is slow to anger is better than the mighty;
      and he that ruleth his spirit
         than he that taketh a city.

25:28 He that hath no rule over his own spirit
      is like a city that is broken down,
         and without walls.

12:16 A fool's wrath is presently known:
      but a prudent man covereth shame.

B. Defuse Anger in Others

15:1 A soft answer turneth away wrath:
      but grievous words stir up anger.

29:8 Scornful men bring a city into a snare:
      but wise men turn away wrath.

16:14 The wrath of a king is as messengers of death:
      but a wise man will pacify it.

C. Stay Away From Angry People

22:24 Make no friendship with an angry man;
      and with a furious man thou shalt not go:
  25 Lest thou learn his ways, and get a snare to thy soul.

Chapter 9

Powerful Words and Speech

*Death and life are in the power of the tongue:
and they that love it shall eat the fruit thereof.*

(18:21)

Page

Pure and Constructive Speech............................94

Controlled Speech 96

Truthful Versus Deceitful Speech 98

Perverse and Harmful Speech 100

PURE AND CONSTRUCTIVE SPEECH

I. A Believer's Speech Should Be Pure and Constructive

A. To Evidence His Converted Heart

10:20   The tongue of the just is as choice silver:
        the heart of the wicked is little worth.

16:23   The heart of the wise teacheth his mouth,
        and addeth learning to his lips.

15:26   The thoughts of the wicked are an abomination
            to the Lord:
        but the words of the pure are pleasant words.

B. To Enhance His Spiritual Life

10:11   The mouth of a righteous man is a well of life:
        but violence covereth the mouth of the wicked.

15:4   A wholesome tongue is a tree of life:
        but perverseness therein is a breach in
            [crushes] the spirit.

C. To Share His Wisdom and Knowledge With Others

10:31   The mouth of the just bringeth forth wisdom:
        but the froward tongue shall be cut out.

15:7   The lips of the wise disperse knowledge:
        but the heart of the foolish doeth not so.

18:4   The words of a man's mouth are as deep waters,
        and the wellspring of wisdom as a flowing brook.

10:21   The lips of the righteous feed many:
        but fools die for want of wisdom.

II. Constructive Speech Is Positive and Productive

A. Pleasant Words Encourage Others

16:24   Pleasant words are as an honeycomb,
        sweet to the soul, and health to the bones.

12:25   Heaviness in the heart of man maketh it stoop:
        but a good word maketh it glad.

12:18   There is that speaketh like the piercings of a sword:
        but the tongue of the wise is health.

B. Soft Replies Promote Peace

15:1　A soft answer turneth away wrath:
　　　　but grievous words stir up anger.

C. Kindly Speech Aids Instruction

16:21　The wise in heart shall be called prudent:
　　　　and the sweetness of the lips increaseth learning.

D. Patient and Gentle Speech Is Persuasive

25:15　By long forbearing is a prince persuaded,
　　　　and a soft tongue breaketh the bone.

E. Apt Comments Bring Pleasure and Enjoyment

25:11　A word fitly spoken
　　　　is like apples of gold in pictures of silver.

15:23　A man hath joy by the answer of his mouth:
　　　　and a word spoken in due season, how good is it!

III. **Pure and Constructive Speech Brings Valuable Rewards**

A. Appreciation and Respect From Others

16:13　Righteous lips are the delight of kings;
　　　　and they love him that speaketh right.

24:26　Every man shall kiss his lips
　　　　that giveth a right answer.

B. Personal Satisfaction and Contentment

18:20　A man's belly shall be satisfied with the fruit
　　　　　　of his mouth;
　　　　and with the increase of his lips shall he be filled.

13:2　A man shall eat good by the fruit of his mouth:
　　　　but the soul of the transgressors shall eat violence.

12:14　A man shall be satisfied with good by the fruit
　　　　　　of his mouth:
　　　　and the recompence of a man's hands shall be
　　　　rendered unto him.

IV. **God Uses Men's Speech to Accomplish His Will**

16:1　The preparations of the heart in man,
　　　　and the answer of the tongue, is from the Lord.

16:10   A divine sentence is in the lips of the king:
his mouth transgresseth not in judgment.

CONTROLLED SPEECH

I. The Wise Person Controls His Tongue

A.   He Knows What to Say and How to Say It

15:2   The tongue of the wise useth knowledge aright:
but the mouth of fools poureth out foolishness.

10:32   The lips of the righteous know what is acceptable:
but the mouth of the wicked speaketh frowardness.

15:28   The heart of the righteous studieth to answer:
but the mouth of the wicked poureth out evil things.

B.   He Knows When to Keep Silent

11:12   He that is void of wisdom despiseth his neighbour:
but a man of understanding holdeth his peace.

12:23   A prudent man concealeth knowledge:
but the heart of fools proclaimeth foolishness.

29:11   A fool uttereth all his mind:
but a wise man keepeth it in till afterwards.

17:28   Even a fool when he holdeth his peace,
is counted wise:
and he that shutteth his lips is esteemed a man
of understanding.

C.   As a Result, He Keeps Out of Trouble

21:23   Whoso keepeth his mouth and his tongue
keepeth his soul from troubles.

13:3   He that keepeth his mouth keepeth his life:
but he that openeth wide his lips shall have
destruction.

14:3   In the mouth of the foolish is a rod of pride:
but the lips of the wise shall preserve them.

II. **Learn to Control Your Tongue**

  A. Don't Speak Prematurely

    18:13 He that answereth a matter before he heareth it,
           it is folly and shame unto him.

    29:20 Seest thou a man that is hasty in his words?
           there is more hope of a fool than of him.

  B. Don't Talk Too Much

    17:27 He that hath knowledge spareth his words:
           and a man of understanding is of an excellent spirit.

    10:19 In the multitude of words there wanteth not sin:
           but he that refraineth his lips is wise.

    14:23 In all labour there is profit:
           but the talk of the lips tendeth only to penury.

  C. Don't Use Inappropriate Speech

    1. Boasting

    27:2 Let another man praise thee, and not thine
           own mouth;
       a stranger, and not thine own lips.

    27:1 Boast not thyself of tomorrow;
           for thou knowest not what a day may bring forth.

    25:14 Whoso boasteth himself of a false gift
           is like clouds and wind without rain.

    20:6 Most men will proclaim every one his own goodness:
           but a faithful man who can find?

    2. Critical and Offensive Comments

    30:10 Accuse not a servant unto his master,
           lest he curse thee, and thou be found guilty.

    25:23 The north wind driveth away rain:
           so doth an angry countenance a backbiting tongue.

    3. Thoughtless and Untimely Statements

    27:14 He that blesseth his friend with a loud voice,
           rising early in the morning,
         it shall be counted a curse to him.

4. Arguing Publicly and Breaking Confidences

25:9   Debate thy cause with thy neighbour himself;
and discover not a secret to another:

10   Lest he that heareth it put thee to shame,
and thine infamy turn not away.

TRUTHFUL VERSUS DECEITFUL SPEECH

I. God Requires Truthfulness

A. God Loves Truthful Speech

3:3   Let not mercy and truth forsake thee:
bind them about thy neck;
write them upon the table of thine heart:

4   So shalt thou find favour and good understanding
in the sight of God and man.

12:22   Lying lips are abomination to the Lord:
but they that deal truly are his delight.

B. God Hates Deceitful Speech

6:16   These six things doth the Lord hate:
yea, seven are an abomination unto him:

17   A proud look, a lying tongue,
and hands that shed innocent blood, . . .

19   A false witness that speaketh lies,
and he that soweth discord among brethren.

II. Truthfulness Is a Spiritual Indicator

A. Godly People Tell the Truth

12:17   He that speaketh truth sheweth forth righteousness:
but a false witness deceit.

13:5   A righteous man hateth lying:
but a wicked man is loathsome, and cometh
to shame.

B. Sinful People Are Susceptible to Lying

17:4   A wicked doer giveth heed to false lips;
and a liar giveth ear to a naughty tongue.

14:5   A faithful witness will not lie:
        but a false witness will utter lies.

14:25   A true witness delivereth souls:
        but a deceitful witness speaketh lies.

10:18   He that hideth hatred with lying lips,
        and he that uttereth a slander, is a fool.

III. Some Lies Are Particularly Damaging

A.   Lies Against Innocent People

25:18   A man that beareth false witness against
        his neighbour
        is a maul, and a sword, and a sharp arrow.

B.   Lies by Those in Leadership

17:7   Excellent speech becometh not a fool:
        much less do lying lips a prince.

29:12   If a ruler hearken to lies,
        all his servants are [become] wicked.

C.   Lies to Obtain Wealth and Possessions

21:6   The getting of treasures by a lying tongue
        is a vanity tossed to and fro of them
        that seek death.

19:22   The desire of a man is his kindness:
        and a poor man is better than a liar.

IV. In the End, Justice Will Be Done

A.   Truthful People Will Prevail

12:19   The lip of truth shall be established for ever:
        but a lying tongue is but for a moment.

B.   Liars Will Be Punished

19:5   A false witness shall not be unpunished,
        and he that speaketh lies shall not escape.

19:9   A false witness shall not be unpunished,
        and he that speaketh lies shall perish.

22:28   A false witness shall perish:
        but the man that heareth speaketh constantly.

V. Determine to Be Truthful

24:28   Be not a witness against thy neighbour
   without cause;
  and deceive not with thy lips.

30:8   Remove far from me vanity and lies:
  give me neither poverty nor riches;
  feed me with food convenient for me:

9   Lest I be full, and deny thee,
  and say, Who is the Lord?
  or lest I be poor, and steal,
  and take the name of my God in vain.

PERVERSE AND HARMFUL SPEECH

I. Perverse Speech Can Do Great Harm

18:21   Death and life are in the power of the tongue:
  and they that love it shall eat the fruit thereof.

12:6   The words of the wicked are to lie in wait for blood:
  but the mouth of the upright shall deliver them.

16:27   An ungodly man diggeth up evil:
  and in his lips there is as a burning fire.

II. Gossip Destroys Relationships

A. Gossip Ruins Friendships

17:9   He that covereth a transgression seeketh love;
  but he that repeateth a matter separateth
   very friends.

16:28   A froward man soweth strife:
  and a whisperer separateth chief friends.

B. Gossip Causes Strife

26:20   Where no wood is, there the fire goeth out:
  so where there is no talebearer, the strife ceaseth.

C. Gossip Betrays Confidences

11:13 A talebearer revealeth secrets:
　　　but he that is of a faithful spirit concealeth
　　　　the matter.

20:19 He that goeth about as a talebearer
　　　　revealeth secrets:
　　　therefore meddle not with him that flattereth
　　　　with his lips.

D. Gossip Cuts Deeply

18:8 The words of a talebearer are as wounds,
　　　and they go down into the innermost parts
　　　　of the belly.

26:22 The words of a talebearer are as wounds,
　　　and they go down into the innermost parts
　　　　of the belly.

III. Flattery Seduces the Gullible

29:5 A man that flattereth his neighbour
　　　spreadeth a net for his feet.

26:28 A lying tongue hateth those that are afflicted by it;
　　　and a flattering mouth worketh ruin.

2:16 To deliver thee from the strange woman,
　　　even from the stranger which flattereth
　　　　with her words; . . .

18 For her house inclineth unto death,
　　　and her paths unto the dead.

6:24 To keep thee from the evil woman,
　　　from the flattery of the tongue of a strange woman.

7:21 With her much fair speech she caused him to yield,
　　　with the flattering of her lips she forced him.

IV. Hypocritical Speech Subverts the Unwary

11:9 An hypocrite with his mouth destroyeth
　　　his neighbour:
　　　but through knowledge shall the just be delivered.

26:23 Burning lips and a wicked heart
      are like a potsherd covered with silver dross.
  24 He that hateth dissembleth with his lips,
      and layeth up deceit within him;
  25 When he speaketh fair, believe him not:
      for there are seven abominations in his heart.

V. God Hates Perverse and Harmful Speech

8:13 The fear of the Lord is to hate evil:
      pride, and arrogancy, and the evil way,
      and the froward mouth, do I hate.

VI. Perverse Speech Harms the Speaker

17:20 He that hath a froward heart findeth no good:
      and he that hath a perverse tongue falleth
      into mischief.

VII. Avoid All Perverse and Harmful Speech

4:24 Put away from thee a froward mouth,
      and perverse lips put far from thee.

19:1 Better is the poor that walketh in his integrity,
      than he that is perverse in his lips, and is a fool.

Chapter 10

Godly Character in Action

She stretcheth out her hand to the poor;
 yea, she reacheth forth her hands to the needy. . . .
Strength and honour are her clothing;
 and she shall rejoice in time to come.
She openeth her mouth with wisdom;
 and in her tongue is the law of kindness.

(31:20, 25-26)

Page

Love and Kindness 104

Generosity 106

Faithfulness 107

Peace With Others Versus Strife 110

Honor and Respect 113

LOVE AND KINDNESS

I. Love One Another

A. Love Your Family

15:17 Better is a dinner of herbs where love is,
       than a stalled ox and hatred therewith.

17:1   Better is a dry morsel, and quietness therewith,
       than an house full of sacrifices [feasting] with strife.

B. Love Your Wife

5:18   Let thy fountain be blessed:
       and rejoice with the wife of thy youth.

19   Let her be as the loving hind and pleasant roe [doe];
       let her breasts satisfy thee at all times;
       and be thou ravished always with her love.

C. Love Your Children

4:3   For I was my father's son,
       tender and only beloved in the sight of my mother.

4   He taught me also, and said unto me,
       Let thine heart retain my words:
       keep my commandments, and live.

3:12   For whom the Lord loveth he correcteth;
       even as a father the son in whom he delighteth.

13:24 He that spareth his rod hateth his son:
       but he that loveth him chasteneth him betimes.

D. Love Your Friends

17:17 A friend loveth at all times,
       and a brother is born for adversity.

II. Demonstrate Your Love

A. Through Kindness

19:22 The desire of a man is his kindness:
       and a poor man is better than a liar.

31:26 She openeth her mouth with wisdom;
       and in her tongue is the law of kindness.

B. Through Forgiveness

17:9 He that covereth a transgression seeketh love;
but he that repeateth a matter separateth
very friends.

10:12 Hatred stirreth up strifes:
but love covereth all sins.

C. Through Loving Constructive Criticism

27:5 Open rebuke is better than secret love.
6 Faithful are the wounds of a friend;
but the kisses of an enemy are deceitful.

III. **Be Kind to Those Who Oppose You**

A. Respond With Genuine Kindness

25:21 If thine enemy be hungry, give him bread to eat;
and if he be thirsty, give him water to drink:
22 For thou shalt heap coals of fire upon his head,
and the Lord shall reward thee.

B. Don't Respond in Vengeance

24:29 Say not, I will do so to him as he hath done to me:
I will render to the man according to his work.

20:22 Say not thou, I will recompense evil;
but wait on the Lord, and he shall save thee.

C. Don't Be Glad at Their Trouble

24:17 Rejoice not when thine enemy falleth,
and let not thine heart be glad when he stumbleth:
18 Lest the Lord see it, and it displease him,
and he turn away his wrath from him.

17:5 Whoso mocketh the poor reproacheth his Maker:
and he that is glad at calamities
shall not be unpunished.

IV. **Be Kind to Animals**

12:10 A righteous man regardeth the life of his beast:
but the tender mercies of the wicked are cruel.

V. **The Kind and Merciful Person Will Be Blessed**

3:3   Let not mercy and truth forsake thee:
    bind them about thy neck;
    write them upon the table of thine heart:

4   So shalt thou find favour and good understanding
    in the sight of God and man.

21:21   He that followeth after righteousness and mercy
    findeth life, righteousness, and honour.

11:17   The merciful man doeth good to his own soul:
    but he that is cruel troubleth his own flesh.

GENEROSITY

I. **Be Generous**

A.   Generosity Is Commanded by God

3:27   Withhold not good from them to whom it is due,
    when it is in the power of thine hand to do it.

28   Say not unto thy neighbour,
    Go, and come again, and tomorrow I will give;
    when thou hast it by thee.

B.   Generosity Honors God

14:31   He that oppresseth the poor reproacheth his Maker:
    but he that honoureth him hath mercy on the poor.

C.   Generosity Is Characteristic of Believers

21:25   The desire of the slothful killeth him;
    for his hands refuse to labour.

26   He coveteth greedily all the day long:
    but the righteous giveth and spareth not.

31:20   She stretcheth out her hand to the poor;
    yea, she reacheth forth her hands to the needy.

II. **God Rewards the Generous Person**

A.   With Happiness and Satisfaction

14:21   He that despiseth his neighbour sinneth:
    but he that hath mercy on the poor, happy is he.

22:9   He that hath a bountiful eye shall be blessed;
    for he giveth of his bread to the poor.

B. With Prosperity and Success

11:24   There is that scattereth, and yet increaseth;
    and there is that withholdeth more than is meet,
      but it tendeth to poverty.
25   The liberal soul shall be made fat:
    and he that watereth shall be watered also himself.

19:17   He that hath pity upon the poor lendeth
    unto the Lord;
    and that which he hath given will he pay
      him again.

III. Selfishness Is Destructive

A. It Produces an Empty, Troubled Life

28:27   He that giveth unto the poor shall not lack:
    but he that hideth his eyes shall have many a curse.

18:1   Through [selfish] desire a man, having separated
    himself,
    seeketh and intermeddleth with [defies] all wisdom.

B. It Brings a Similar Response From Others

21:13   Whoso stoppeth his ears at the cry of the poor,
    he also shall cry himself, but shall not be heard.

FAITHFULNESS

I. Be Faithful to God

A. Be Faithful to God's Word

6:20   My son, keep thy father's commandment,
    and forsake not the law of thy mother:
21   Bind them continually upon thine heart,
    and tie them about thy neck.

B. Be Faithful to Godly Principles

4:23   Keep thy heart with all diligence;
    for out of it are the issues of life. . . .

25 Let thine eyes look right on,
     and let thine eyelids look straight before thee. . . .
27 Turn not to the right hand nor to the left:
     remove thy foot from evil.

C. Be Faithful Before Unbelievers

25:26 A righteous man falling down before the wicked
        is as a troubled fountain, and a corrupt spring.

28:4 They that forsake the law praise the wicked:
       but such as keep the law contend with them.

II. **Be Faithful to Others**

A. Be Faithful to Your Spouse

31:10 Who can find a virtuous woman?
        for her price is far above rubies.
  11 The heart of her husband doth safely trust in her,
       so that he shall have no need of spoil.
  12 She will do him good and not evil
       all the days of her life.

5:18 Let thy fountain be blessed:
       and rejoice with the wife of thy youth. . . .
  20 And why wilt thou, my son, be ravished
         with a strange woman,
       and embrace the bosom of a stranger?

B. Be Faithful to Those in Authority Over You

25:13 As the cold of snow in the time of harvest,
        so is a faithful messenger to them that send him:
        for he refresheth the soul of his masters.

13:17 A wicked messenger falleth into mischief:
        but a faithful ambassador is health.

C. Be Faithful to Your Friends

27:10 Thine own friend, and thy father's friend,
          forsake not;
        neither go into thy brother's house in the day
          of thy calamity:
        for better is a neighbour that is near
          than a brother far off.

27:6 Faithful are the wounds [rebukes] of a friend;
but the kisses of an enemy are deceitful.

18:24 A man that hath friends must shew himself friendly:
and there is a friend that sticketh closer
than a brother.

D. Be Faithful to Those Who Confide in You

11:13 A talebearer revealeth secrets:
but he that is of a faithful spirit concealeth
the matter.

III. Be Faithful to Your Responsibilities

27:23 Be thou diligent to know the state of thy flocks,
and look well to thy herds.

31:27 She looketh well to the ways of her household,
and eateth not the bread of idleness.

IV. Be Faithful in Spite of Adversity

24:10 If thou faint in the day of adversity,
thy strength is small.

24:16 For a just man falleth seven times, and riseth
up again:
but the wicked shall fall into mischief.

18:14 The spirit of a man will sustain his infirmity;
but a wounded spirit who can bear?

V. Be Faithful in All Things

A. A Faithful Person Is Hard to Find

20:6 Most men will proclaim every one his own goodness:
but a faithful man who can find?

B. A Faithful Person Will Be Blessed

28:20 A faithful man shall abound with blessings:
but he that maketh haste to be rich
shall not be innocent.

C. An Unfaithful Person Hurts Others

25:19 Confidence in an unfaithful man in time of trouble
is like a broken tooth, and a foot out of joint.

PEACE WITH OTHERS VERSUS STRIFE

I. Seek Peace With Others

A. Peace With Others Is Better Than Riches

17:1   Better is a dry morsel, and quietness therewith,
         than an house full of sacrifices with strife.

B. God Arranges Peaceful Relationships for Those
    Who Please Him

16:7   When a man's ways please the Lord,
         he maketh even his enemies to be at peace
         with him.

C. God Hates Those Who Foster Strife

6:16   These six things doth the Lord hate:
         yea, seven are an abomination unto him: . . .

19   A false witness that speaketh lies,
         and he that soweth discord among brethren.

II. Promote Peace With Others

A. With Self-Control and Patience

15:18   A wrathful man stirreth up strife:
         but he that is slow to anger appeaseth strife.

B. With Gentle Speech

15:1   A soft answer turneth away wrath:
         but grievous words stir up anger.

25:15   By long forbearing is a prince persuaded,
         and a soft tongue breaketh the bone.

C. With Appropriate Tolerance

19:11   The discretion of a man deferreth his anger;
         and it is his glory to pass over a transgression.

D. By Encouraging Reconciliation

12:20   Deceit is in the heart of them that imagine evil:
         but to the counsellors of peace is joy.

E. By Avoiding Disagreements

20:3   It is an honour for a man to cease from strife:
         but every fool will be meddling.

F. With Impartial Settlement of Disputes

18:18   The lot causeth contentions to cease,
and parteth between the mighty.

III. Avoid Attitudes and Dispositions That Lead to Strife

A. Pride

28:25   He that is of a proud heart stirreth up strife:
but he that putteth his trust in the Lord
shall be made fat.

13:10   Only by pride cometh contention:
but with the well advised is wisdom.

B. Anger

29:22   An angry man stirreth up strife,
and a furious man aboundeth in transgression.

30:33   Surely the churning of milk bringeth forth butter,
and the wringing of the nose bringeth forth blood:
so the forcing of wrath bringeth forth strife.

C. Hatred

10:12   Hatred stirreth up strifes:
but love covereth all sins.

IV. Avoid People That Cause Strife

A. Contentious People

26:21   As coals are to burning coals, and wood to fire;
so is a contentious man to kindle strife.

21:9   It is better to dwell in a corner of the housetop,
than with a brawling woman in a wide house.

B. Gossips

26:20   Where no wood is, there the fire goeth out:
so where there is no talebearer, the strife ceaseth.

16:28   A froward man soweth strife:
and a whisperer separateth chief friends.

C. Sinful People

17:19   He loveth transgression that loveth strife:
and he that exalteth his gate seeketh destruction.

D. Fools (Those Who Disregard God)

20:3   It is an honour for a man to cease from strife:
        but every fool will be meddling.

18:6   A fool's lips enter into contention,
        and his mouth calleth for strokes [a beating].

E. Scoffers (Those Who Mock God)

22:10   Cast out the scorner, and contention shall go out;
        yea, strife and reproach shall cease.

V. Avoid Situations That Cause Strife

A. Don't Start Arguments

25:8   Go not forth hastily to strive,
        lest thou know not what to do in the end thereof,
        when thy neighbour hath put thee to shame.

17:14   The beginning of strife is as when one letteth
            out water:
        therefore leave off contention, before it be
            meddled with.

3:30   Strive not with a man without cause,
        if he have done thee no harm.

B. Stay Out of Others' Arguments

26:17   He that passeth by, and meddleth with strife
            belonging not to him,
        is like one that taketh a dog by the ears.

C. Don't Offend a Brother

18:19   A brother offended is harder to be won
            than a strong city:
        and their contentions are like the bars of a castle.

D. Don't Argue With a Fool

29:9   If a wise man contendeth with a foolish man,
        whether he rage or laugh, there is no rest.

HONOR AND RESPECT

I. **God Honors the True Believer**

A.   Who Honors God in His Heart

22:4   By humility and the fear of the Lord
are riches, and honour, and life.

31:30   Favour is deceitful, and beauty is vain:
but a woman that feareth the Lord,
she shall be praised.

B.   Who Honors God by His Righteous Life

21:21   He that followeth after righteousness and mercy
findeth life, righteousness, and honour.

12:2   A good man obtaineth favour of the Lord:
but a man of wicked devices will he condemn.

C.   Who Honors God With His Possessions

3:9   Honour the Lord with thy substance,
and with the firstfruits of all thine increase:

10   So shall thy barns be filled with plenty,
and thy presses shall burst out with new wine.

14:31   He that oppresseth the poor reproacheth his Maker:
but he that honoureth him hath mercy on the poor.

II. **Desirable Traits Bring Honor and Respect**

A.   Humility

15:33   The fear of the Lord is the instruction of wisdom;
and before honour is humility.

18:12   Before destruction the heart of man is haughty,
and before honour is humility.

29:23   A man's pride shall bring him low:
but honour shall uphold the humble in spirit.

B.   Wisdom

3:35   The wise shall inherit glory:
but shame shall be the promotion of fools.

12:8   A man shall be commended according to his wisdom:
but he that is of a perverse heart shall be despised.

13:15   Good understanding giveth favour:
   but the way of transgressors is hard.

4:7   Wisdom is the principal thing; therefore get wisdom:
   and with all thy getting get understanding.

8   Exalt her, and she shall promote thee:
   she shall bring thee to honour,
    when thou dost embrace her.

9   She shall give to thine head an ornament of grace:
   a crown of glory shall she deliver to thee.

3:16   Length of days is in her right hand;
   and in her left hand riches and honour.

C.   Kindness and Truthfulness

3:3   Let not mercy and truth forsake thee:
   bind them about thy neck;
   write them upon the table of thine heart:

4   So shalt thou find favour and good understanding
   in the sight of God and man.

D.   Graciousness

11:16   A gracious woman retaineth honour:
   and strong men retain riches.

E.   Avoidance of Strife

20:3   It is an honour for a man to cease from strife:
   but every fool will be meddling.

F.   Diligence in Good Works

11:27   He that diligently seeketh good procureth favour:
   but he that seeketh mischief, it shall come
    unto him.

31:27   She looketh well to the ways of her household,
   and eateth not the bread of idleness.

28   Her children arise up, and call her blessed;
   her husband also, and he praiseth her.

29   Many daughters have done virtuously,
   but thou excellest them all. . . .

31   Give her of the fruit of her hands;
   and let her own works praise her in the gates.

G. Faithfulness in Service

27:18 Whoso keepeth the fig tree shall eat the fruit thereof:
       so he that waiteth on his master shall be honoured.

14:35 The king's favour is toward a wise servant:
       but his wrath is against him that causeth shame.

H. Responsiveness to Correction

13:18 Poverty and shame shall be to him that refuseth
       instruction:
       but he that regardeth reproof shall be honoured.

Chapter 11

The Successful Home and Family

*The curse of the Lord is in the house of the wicked:
but he blesseth the habitation of the just.*

(3:33)

	Page
The Home	118
Men and Husbands	119
Women and Wives	121
Parents and Children	124
Sons and Daughters	127

THE HOME

I. God's Blueprint for a Successful Home

A. Careful Planning and Preparation

24:27   Prepare thy work without,
and make it fit for thyself in the field;
and afterwards build thine house.

B. Wise Management and Operation

24:3   Through wisdom is an house builded;
and by understanding it is established:
4   And by knowledge shall the chambers be filled
with all precious and pleasant riches.

14:1   Every wise woman buildeth her house:
but the foolish plucketh it down with her hands.

C. Godly, Upright Living

2:21   For the upright shall dwell in the land,
and the perfect shall remain in it.

14:19   The evil bow before the good;
and the wicked at the gates of the righteous.

D. Promotion of Love and Peace

15:17   Better is a dinner of herbs where love is,
than a stalled ox and hatred therewith.

17:1   Better is a dry morsel, and quietness therewith,
than an house full of sacrifices with strife.

E. Avoidance of Wrong Behavior

11:29   He that troubleth his own house shall inherit
the wind:
and the fool shall be servant to the wise of heart.

15:27   He that is greedy of gain troubleth his own house;
but he that hateth gifts shall live.

17:13   Whoso rewardeth evil for good,
evil shall not depart from his house.

II. **God's Blessing for a Righteous Home**

  A. Prosperity and Success

    14:11 The house of the wicked shall be overthrown:
          but the tabernacle of the upright shall flourish.

    3:33 The curse of the Lord is in the house of the wicked:
          but he blesseth the habitation of the just.

    15:6 In the house of the righteous is much treasure:
          but in the revenues of the wicked is trouble.

    21:20 There is treasure to be desired and oil
          in the dwelling of the wise;
          but a foolish man spendeth it up.

  B. Stability and Endurance

    12:7 The wicked are overthrown, and are not:
          but the house of the righteous shall stand.

  C. Protection and Security

    24:15 Lay not wait, O wicked man, against the dwelling
          of the righteous;
          spoil not his resting place:

    16 For a just man falleth seven times,
          and riseth up again:
          but the wicked shall fall into mischief.

    15:25 The Lord will destroy the house of the proud:
          but he will establish the border of the widow.

MEN AND HUSBANDS

I. **A Good Husband**

  A. He Is Faithful to His Wife

    5:15 Drink waters out of thine own cistern,
          and running waters out of thine own well.

    16 Let thy fountains be dispersed abroad,
          and rivers of waters in the streets. (Or, "Why let. . .?")

    17 Let them be only thine own,
          and not strangers' with thee. . . .

20 And why wilt thou, my son,
 be ravished with a strange woman,
 and embrace the bosom of a stranger?

B. He Shares Intimate Love With His Wife

5:18 Let thy fountain be blessed:
 and rejoice with the wife of thy youth.
19 Let her be as the loving hind and pleasant roe [doe];
 let her breasts satisfy thee at all times;
 and be thou ravished always with her love.

C. He Appreciates and Praises His Wife

31:28 Her children arise up, and call her blessed;
 her husband also, and he praiseth her.

II. A Good Father (See also "Parents and Children")

A. He Is the Pride of His Children

17:6 Children's children are the crown of old men;
 and the glory of children are their fathers.

B. He Provides for His Descendents

19:14 House and riches are the inheritance of fathers:
 and a prudent wife is from the Lord.

13:22 A good man leaveth an inheritance to his
  children's children:
 and the wealth of the sinner is laid up for the just.

III. Older Men

A. They Earn Honor and Respect Through Godly Lives

16:31 The hoary [gray] head is a crown of glory,
 if it be found in the way of righteousness.

20:29 The glory of young men is their strength:
 and the beauty of old men is the gray head.

B. They Are Blessed by Their Grandchildren

17:6 Children's children are the crown of old men;
 and the glory of children are their fathers.

WOMEN AND WIVES

I. **Commendable Women**

A. A Wise Woman Is Constructive

14:1 Every wise woman buildeth her house:
 but the foolish plucketh it down with her hands.

B. A Gracious Woman Earns Respect

11:16 A gracious woman retaineth honour:
 and strong men retain riches.

II. **Disgraceful Women**

A. A Contentious Woman Is Unbearable

27:15 A continual dropping in a very rainy day
 and a contentious woman are alike.
 16 Whosoever hideth her hideth the wind,
 and the ointment of his right hand, which
 bewrayeth itself [grasps oil with his hand].

19:13 A foolish son is the calamity of his father:
 and the contentions of a wife are a
 continual dropping.

25:24 It is better to dwell in the corner of the housetop,
 than with a brawling woman and in a wide house.

21:9 It is better to dwell in a corner of the housetop,
 than with a brawling woman in a wide house.

21:19 It is better to dwell in the wilderness,
 than with a contentious and an angry woman.

B. An Indiscreet Woman Is Shameful

11:22 As a jewel of gold in a swine's snout,
 so is a fair woman which is without discretion.

C. An Aggressive Woman Is Offensive

30:21 For three things the earth is disquieted,
 and for four which it cannot bear: . . .
 23 For an odious woman when she is married;
 and an handmaid that is heir to her mistress.

D.   An Adulterous Woman Is Treacherous

   2:16   To deliver thee from the strange woman,
          even from the stranger which flattereth with
          her words;

    17   Which forsaketh the guide [partner] of her youth,
         and forgetteth the covenant of her God.

    18   For her house inclineth unto death,
         and her paths unto the dead.

    19   None that go unto her return again,
         neither take they hold of the paths of life.

III. **A Barren Woman**

  30:15   The horseleach hath two daughters, crying,
         Give, give.
        There are three things that are never satisfied,
        yea, four things say not, It is enough.

    16   The grave; and the barren womb;
         the earth that is not filled with water;
         and the fire that saith not, It is enough.

IV. **A Good Wife**

A.   She Is God's Gift to Her Husband

  18:22   Whoso findeth a wife findeth a good thing,
         and obtaineth favour of the Lord.

  19:14   House and riches are the inheritance of fathers:
         and a prudent wife is from the Lord.

B.   She Honors and Encourages Her Husband

  31:10   Who can find a virtuous woman?
         for her price is far above rubies.

    11   The heart of her husband doth safely trust in her,
         so that he shall have no need of spoil.

    12   She will do him good and not evil
         all the days of her life.

  31:23   Her husband is known in the gates,
         when he sitteth among the elders of the land.

C. She Faithfully Cares for her Family

   1. She Feeds Them Well

31:14 She is like the merchants' ships;
       she bringeth her food from afar.
   15 She riseth also while it is yet night,
       and giveth meat to her household,
       and a portion to her maidens.

   2. She Clothes Them Well

31:21 She is not afraid of the snow for her household:
       for all her household are clothed with scarlet.
   22 She maketh herself coverings of tapestry;
       her clothing is silk and purple.

   3. She Cares for All Their Needs

31:27 She looketh well to the ways of her household,
       and eateth not the bread of idleness.

D. She Works Diligently and Intelligently

31:16 She considereth a field, and buyeth it:
       with the fruit of her hands she planteth a vineyard.
   17 She girdeth her loins with strength,
       and strengtheneth her arms.
   18 She perceiveth that her merchandise is good:
       her candle goeth not out by night.
   19 She layeth her hands to the spindle,
       and her hands hold the distaff.

31:13 She seeketh wool, and flax,
       and worketh willingly with her hands. . . .
   24 She maketh fine linen, and selleth it;
       and delivereth girdles unto the merchant.

E. She Is Kind and Noble

31:20 She stretcheth out her hand to the poor;
       yea, she reacheth forth her hands to the needy. . . .
   25 Strength and honour are her clothing;
       and she shall rejoice in time to come.
   26 She openeth her mouth with wisdom;
       and in her tongue is the law of kindness.

F.　She Is Honored by Her Family

31:28　Her children arise up, and call her blessed;
　　　　her husband also, and he praiseth her.

　29　Many daughters have done virtuously,
　　　　but thou excellest them all.

G.　She Is Honored Throughout the Community

31:30　Favour is deceitful, and beauty is vain:
　　　　but a woman that feareth the Lord,
　　　　　she shall be praised.

　31　Give her of the fruit of her hands;
　　　　and let her own works praise her in the gates.

PARENTS AND CHILDREN

I. Parental Responsibilities

A.　Train Your Children at an Early Age

22:6　Train up a child in the way he should go:
　　　　and when he is old, he will not depart from it.

20:11　Even a child is known by his doings,
　　　　whether his work be pure, and whether it be right.

B.　Lovingly Instruct Them in Doctrine and Holy Living

4:1　Hear, ye children, the instruction of a father,
　　　　and attend to know understanding.

　2　For I give you good doctrine,
　　　　forsake ye not my law.

　3　For I was my father's son,
　　　　tender and only beloved in the sight of my mother.

　4　He taught me also, and said unto me,
　　　　Let thine heart retain my words:
　　　　keep my commandments, and live.

31:1　The words of king Lemuel,
　　　　the prophecy that his mother taught him.

　2　What, my son? and what, the son of my womb?
　　　　and what, the son of my vows?

　3　Give not thy strength unto women,
　　　　nor thy ways to that which destroyeth kings.

C. Lead Them by Your Godly Example

23:26 My son, give me thine heart,
and let thine eyes observe my ways.

20:7 The just man walketh in his integrity:
his children are blessed after him.

14:26 In the fear of the Lord is strong confidence:
and his children shall have a place of refuge.

D. Correct and Discipline Your Children

1. In Love and With Consistency

13:24 He that spareth his rod hateth his son:
but he that loveth him chasteneth him betimes.

3:11 My son, despise not the chastening of the Lord;
neither be weary of his correction:

12 For whom the Lord loveth he correcteth;
even as a father the son in whom he delighteth.

2. To Increase Their Wisdom

29:15 The rod and reproof give wisdom:
but a child left to himself bringeth his mother
to shame.

22:15 Foolishness is bound in the heart of a child;
but the rod of correction shall drive it
far from him.

3. For Their Future Protection

23:13 Withhold not correction from the child:
for if thou beatest him with the rod,
he shall not die.

14 Thou shalt beat him with the rod,
and shalt deliver his soul from hell.

19:18 Chasten thy son while there is hope,
and let not thy soul spare for his crying.

II. **Parental Results and Rewards**

A. Wise Children Bring Their Parents Happiness

10:1 The proverbs of Solomon.
A wise son maketh a glad father:
but a foolish son is the heaviness of his mother.

15:20 A wise son maketh a glad father:
but a foolish man despiseth his mother.

23:15 My son, if thine heart be wise,
my heart shall rejoice, even mine.

16 Yea, my reins [inmost being] shall rejoice,
when thy lips speak right things.

27:11 My son, be wise, and make my heart glad,
that I may answer him that reproacheth me.

B. Righteous Children Bring Them Joy

23:24 The father of the righteous shall greatly rejoice:
and he that begetteth a wise child shall have joy
of him.

25 Thy father and thy mother shall be glad,
and she that bare thee shall rejoice.

C. Disciplined Children Bring Them Contentment

29:17 Correct thy son, and he shall give thee rest;
yea, he shall give delight unto thy soul.

D. Undisciplined Children Bring Them Shame

29:15 The rod and reproof give wisdom:
but a child left to himself bringeth his mother
to shame.

E. Foolish Children Bring Them Grief

17:25 A foolish son is a grief to his father,
and bitterness to her that bare him.

17:21 He that begetteth a fool doeth it to his sorrow:
and the father of a fool hath no joy.

19:13 A foolish son is the calamity of his father:
and the contentions of a wife are a
continual dropping.

SONS AND DAUGHTERS

I. Value Your Parents' Instruction and Advice

A. Listen to Your Parents

23:22   Hearken unto thy father that begat thee,
       and despise not thy mother when she is old.

13:1   A wise son heareth his father's instruction:
       but a scorner heareth not rebuke.

15:5   A fool despiseth his father's instruction:
       but he that regardeth reproof is prudent.

B. Obtain Wisdom and Knowledge From Them

5:1   My son, attend unto my wisdom,
       and bow thine ear to my understanding:
2   That thou mayest regard discretion,
       and that thy lips may keep knowledge.

23:19   Hear thou, my son, and be wise,
       and guide thine heart in the way.

II. Benefit From Your Parents' Instruction

A. It Will Help You Know God Better

2:1   My son, if thou wilt receive my words,
       and hide my commandments with thee; . . .
5   Then shalt thou understand the fear of the Lord,
       and find the knowledge of God.

B. It Will Guide and Protect You

6:20   My son, keep thy father's commandment,
       and forsake not the law of thy mother: . . .
22   When thou goest, it shall lead thee;
       when thou sleepest, it shall keep thee;
       and when thou wakest, it shall talk with thee.

C. It Will Enhance the Quality of Your Life

4:20   My son, attend to my words;
       incline thine ear unto my sayings. . . .
22   For they are life unto those that find them,
       and health to all their flesh.

D. It Will Give You a Long, Peaceful Life

3:1   My son, forget not my law;
         but let thine heart keep my commandments:

2   For length of days, and long life,
         and peace, shall they add to thee.

III. **Respect and Honor Your Parents**

A. Disrespect of Parents Is Shameful

19:26 He that wasteth [robs] his father, and chaseth away
             his mother,
         is a son that causeth shame, and bringeth reproach.

28:24 Whoso robbeth his father or his mother, and saith,
             It is no transgression;
         the same is the companion of a destroyer.

B. Disrespect Leads to Arrogance and Rebellion

30:11 There is a generation that curseth their father,
             and doth not bless their mother.

12   There is a generation that are pure in their own eyes,
             and yet is not washed from their filthiness.

13   There is a generation, O how lofty are their eyes!
             and their eyelids are lifted up.

14   There is a generation, whose teeth are as swords,
             and their jaw teeth as knives,
         to devour the poor from off the earth,
             and the needy from among men.

C. Disrespect Will Bring Severe Punishment From God

20:20 Whoso curseth his father or his mother,
             his lamp shall be put out in obscure darkness.

30:17 The eye that mocketh at his father,
             and despiseth to obey his mother,
         the ravens of the valley shall pick it out,
             and the young eagles shall eat it.

Chapter 12

Special Relationships With Others

Iron sharpeneth iron;
so a man sharpeneth the countenance of his friend.

(27:17)

Page

Friends 130

Neighbors 133

Rulers and Leaders 135

Citizens 138

FRIENDS

I. Choose Your Friends Carefully

A. A Friend's Character Affects Your Own

27:17   Iron sharpeneth iron;
      so a man sharpeneth the countenance of his friend.

13:20   He that walketh with wise men shall be wise:
      but a companion of fools shall be destroyed.

B. Good Friends Help You Improve

27:9   Ointment and perfume rejoice the heart:
      so doth the sweetness of a man's friend
        by hearty [earnest] counsel.

27:5   Open rebuke is better than secret love.
  6   Faithful are the wounds of a friend;
      but the kisses of an enemy are deceitful.

C. Harmful Friends Drag You Down

  1. Pleasure-Seekers

23:20   Be not among winebibbers;
      among riotous [gluttonous] eaters of flesh:
  21   For the drunkard and the glutton shall come
        to poverty:
      and drowsiness shall clothe a man with rags.

28:7   Whoso keepeth the law is a wise son:
      but he that is a companion of riotous men
        shameth his father.

28:19   He that tilleth his land shall have plenty of bread:
      but he that followeth after vain persons shall have
        poverty enough.

  2. Bitter and Discontented People

22:24   Make no friendship with an angry man;
      and with a furious man thou shalt not go:
  25   Lest thou learn his ways,
      and get a snare to thy soul.

24:21   My son, fear thou the Lord and the king:
      and meddle not with them that are given to change:

22   For their calamity shall rise suddenly;
and who knoweth the ruin of them both?

3. Crooked People

29:24   Whoso is partner with a thief hateth his own soul:
he heareth cursing [the oath], and bewrayeth [tells]
it not.

4. Fools (Who Disregard God)

14:7   Go from the presence of a foolish man,
when thou perceivest not in him
the lips of knowledge.

5. Immoral People

29:3   Whoso loveth wisdom rejoiceth his father:
but he that keepeth company with harlots
spendeth his substance.

6. Sinful People

24:1   Be not thou envious against evil men,
neither desire to be with them.
2   For their heart studieth destruction,
and their lips talk of mischief.

1:10   My son, if sinners entice thee,
consent thou not.
11   If they say, Come with us,
let us lay wait for blood,
let us lurk privily for the innocent
without cause: . . .
14   Cast in thy lot among us;
let us all have one purse:
15   My son, walk not thou in the way with them;
refrain thy foot from their path:

II. Be True to Your Friends

A. Support Them in Their Need

17:17   A friend loveth at all times,
and a brother is born for adversity.

18:24   A man that hath friends must shew himself friendly:
and there is a friend that sticketh closer
than a brother.

27:10   Thine own friend, and thy father's friend,
forsake not;
neither go into thy brother's house
in the day of thy calamity:
for better is a neighbour that is near
than a brother far off.

B.   Keep Their Confidence

17:9   He that covereth a transgression seeketh love;
but he that repeateth a matter separateth
very friends.

16:28   A froward man soweth strife:
and a whisperer separateth chief friends.

C.   Show Them Respect and Courtesy

27:14   He that blesseth his friend with a loud voice,
rising early in the morning,
it shall be counted a curse to him.

III. Beware of Insincere Friends

19:6   Many will entreat the favour of the prince:
and every man is a friend to him
that giveth gifts.

19:7   All the brethren of the poor do hate him:
how much more do his friends go far from him?
he pursueth them with words,
yet they are wanting to him.

19:4   Wealth maketh many friends;
but the poor is separated from his neighbour.

14:20   The poor is hated even of his own neighbour:
but the rich hath many friends.

IV. Don't Guarantee a Friend's Debts

17:18   A man void of understanding striketh hands,
and becometh surety in the presence of his friend.

6:1 My son, if thou be surety for thy friend,
  if thou hast stricken thy hand with a stranger,
2 Thou art snared with the words of thy mouth,
  thou art taken with the words of thy mouth.
3 Do this now, my son, and deliver thyself,
  when thou art come into the hand of thy friend;
  go, humble thyself, and make sure thy friend.
4 Give not sleep to thine eyes,
  nor slumber to thine eyelids.
5 Deliver thyself as a roe from the hand of the hunter,
  and as a bird from the hand of the fowler.

NEIGHBORS

I. **Be a Good Neighbor**

A. Help Your Neighbor When You Can

3:27 Withhold not good from them to whom it is due,
  when it is in the power of thine hand to do it.
28 Say not unto thy neighbour, Go, and come again,
  and tomorrow I will give;
  when thou hast it by thee.

B. Live Above Reproach Before Him

12:26 The righteous is more excellent than his neighbour:
  but the way of the wicked seduceth them.

18:17 He that is first in his own cause seemeth just;
  but his neighbour cometh and searcheth him.

II. **Seek a Good Relationship With Your Neighbor**

A. Live in Peace With Him

3:29 Devise not evil against thy neighbour,
  seeing he dwelleth securely by thee.
30 Strive not with a man without cause,
  if he have done thee no harm.

24:28 Be not a witness against thy neighbour
  without cause;
  and deceive not with thy lips.

29   Say not, I will do so to him as he hath done to me:
  I will render to the man according to his work.

11:12   He that is void of wisdom despiseth his neighbour:
  but a man of understanding holdeth his peace.

B. Settle Problems With Him Calmly and Privately

25:8 Go not forth hastily to strive,
  lest thou know not what to do in the end thereof,
  when thy neighbour hath put thee to shame.

9 Debate thy cause with thy neighbour himself;
  and discover not a secret to another:

10 Lest he that heareth it put thee to shame,
  and thine infamy turn not away.

C. Don't Linger in His House

25:17   Withdraw thy foot from thy neighbour's house;
  lest he be weary of thee, and so hate thee.

III. Avoid Harmful Neighbors

A. A Flattering Neighbor

29:5 A man that flattereth his neighbour
  spreadeth a net for his feet.

B. A Deceitful Neighbor

26:18   As a mad man who casteth firebrands, arrows,
   and death,

19 So is the man that deceiveth his neighbour,
  and saith, Am not I in sport?

25:18   A man that beareth false witness against
   his neighbour
  is a maul, and a sword, and a sharp arrow.

C. A Wicked Neighbor

21:10   The soul of the wicked desireth evil:
  his neighbour findeth no favour in his eyes.

16:29   A violent man enticeth his neighbour,
  and leadeth him into the way that is not good.

RULERS AND LEADERS

I. **God Works Through Rulers and Leaders**

21:1   The king's heart is in the hand of the Lord,
   as the rivers of water:
 he turneth it whithersoever he will.

16:10   A divine sentence is in the lips of the king:
   his mouth transgresseth not in judgment.

II. **A Leader Has Greater Accountability to God**

A.   Leaders in Particular Must Avoid Sinful Practices

16:12   It is an abomination to kings to commit wickedness:
   for the throne is established by righteousness.

17:7   Excellent speech becometh not a fool:
   much less do lying lips a prince.

31:3   Give not thy strength unto women,
   nor thy ways to that which destroyeth kings.

4   It is not for kings, O Lemuel,
   it is not for kings to drink wine;
   nor for princes strong drink:

5   Lest they drink, and forget the law,
   and pervert the judgment of any of the afflicted.

B.   A Leader's Relationship to God Affects His People

29:2   When the righteous are in authority,
   the people rejoice:
 but when the wicked beareth rule,
   the people mourn.

28:12   When righteous men do rejoice, there is great glory:
   but when the wicked rise, a man is hidden.

28:28   When the wicked rise, men hide themselves:
   but when they perish, the righteous increase.

28:15   As a roaring lion, and a ranging bear;
   so is a wicked ruler over the poor people.

III. **A Leader's Character and Wisdom Determine His Success**

A. A Leader's Integrity Strengthens His Position

20:28 Mercy and truth preserve the king:
and his throne is upholden by mercy.

29:4 The king by judgment establisheth the land:
but he that receiveth gifts overthroweth it.

29:14 The king that faithfully judgeth the poor,
his throne shall be established for ever.

B. A Leader Needs Wisdom to Lead Effectively

8:14 Counsel is mine, and sound wisdom:
I am understanding; I have strength.

15 By me kings reign,
and princes decree justice.

16 By me princes rule, and nobles,
even all the judges of the earth.

28:2 For the transgression of a land many are the
princes thereof:
but by a man of understanding and knowledge
the state thereof shall be prolonged.

C. An Unqualified Leader Causes Turmoil and Dismay

28:16 The prince that wanteth understanding
is also a great oppressor:
but he that hateth covetousness
shall prolong his days.

30:21 For three things the earth is disquieted,
and for four which it cannot bear:

22 For a servant when he reigneth;
and a fool when he is filled with meat; . . .

19:10 Delight is not seemly for a fool;
much less for a servant to have rule over princes.

D. A Leader's Honor Is Related to His Following

14:28 In the multitude of people is the king's honour:
but in the want of people is the destruction
of the prince.

IV. **God Gives Specific Instructions to Leaders**

A. Listen Only to Upright Advisers

29:12 If a ruler hearken to lies,
   all his servants are [become] wicked.

25:4 Take away the dross from the silver,
   and there shall come forth a vessel for the finer.
 5 Take away the wicked from before the king,
   and his throne shall be established in righteousness.

B. Beware of People With Ulterior Motives

19:6 Many will entreat the favour of the prince:
   and every man is a friend to him
    that giveth gifts.

29:26 Many seek the ruler's favour;
   but every man's judgment cometh from the Lord.

C. Thoroughly Examine Important Issues

25:2 It is the glory of God to conceal a thing:
   but the honour of kings is to search out a matter.

D. Be Impartial and Fair in Judgment

24:23 These things also belong to the wise.
   It is not good to have respect of persons
    in judgment.

18:5 It is not good to accept the person of the wicked,
   to overthrow the righteous in judgment.

17:26 Also to punish the just is not good,
   nor to strike princes for equity [their integrity].

E. Defend the Disadvantaged

31:8 Open thy mouth for the dumb
   in the cause of all such as are appointed
    to destruction.
 9 Open thy mouth, judge righteously,
   and plead the cause of the poor and needy.

F. Punish Wrong-Doers

20:26 A wise king scattereth the wicked,
   and bringeth the [threshing] wheel over them.

20:8 A king that sitteth in the throne of judgment
scattereth away all evil with his eyes.

24:24 He that saith unto the wicked, Thou art righteous;
him shall the people curse, nations shall abhor him:
25 But to them that rebuke him shall be delight,
and a good blessing shall come upon them.

17:15 He that justifieth the wicked,
and he that condemneth the just,
even they both are abomination to the Lord.

V. Rulers and Leaders Often Are Inscrutable

25:3 The heaven for height, and the earth for depth,
and the heart of kings is unsearchable.

CITIZENS

I. Citizens Honor or Disgrace Their Nation by Their Character

14:34 Righteousness exalteth a nation:
but sin is a reproach to any people.

11:10 When it goeth well with the righteous,
the city rejoiceth:
and when the wicked perish, there is shouting.
11 By the blessing of the upright the city is exalted:
but it is overthrown by the mouth of the wicked.

29:8 Scornful men bring a city into a snare:
but wise men turn away wrath.

II. Believers Should Be Good Citizens

A. They Respect and Obey Those in Authority

24:21 My son, fear thou the Lord and the king:
and meddle not with them that are given to change:
22 For their calamity shall rise suddenly;
and who knoweth the ruin of them both?

20:2 The fear of a king is as the roaring of a lion:
whoso provoketh him to anger sinneth against
his own soul.

B. They Please Those in Authority by Upright Lives

22:11   He that loveth pureness of heart,
   for the grace of his lips the king shall be
    his friend.

16:13   Righteous lips are the delight of kings;
   and they love him that speaketh right.

16:15   In the light of the king's countenance is life;
   and his favour is as a cloud of the latter rain.

C. They Avoid Antagonizing Those in Authority

16:14   The wrath of a king is as messengers of death:
   but a wise man will pacify it.

19:12   The king's wrath is as the roaring of a lion;
   but his favour is as dew upon the grass.

14:35   The king's favour is toward a wise servant:
   but his wrath is against him that causeth shame.

III. Wise Citizens Conduct Themselves Properly in Their Ruler's Presence

A. They Demonstrate Humility and Deference

25:6   Put not forth thyself in the presence of the king,
   and stand not in the place of great men:
7 For better it is that it be said unto thee,
   Come up hither;
  than that thou shouldest be put lower
   in the presence of the prince
   whom thine eyes have seen.

B. They Use Caution and Restraint

23:1   When thou sittest to eat with a ruler,
   consider diligently what is before thee:
2 And put a knife to thy throat,
   if thou be a man given to appetite.
3 Be not desirous of his dainties:
   for they are deceitful meat.

Chapter 13

Principles for Work and Business

Seest thou a man diligent in his business?
He shall stand before kings;
he shall not stand before mean men.

(22:29)

	Page
Work	142
Laziness	144
Business Principles	146
Financial Practices	149

WORK

I. **Work Is Necessary to Satisfy Physical Needs**

16:26   He that laboureth laboureth for himself;
      for his mouth craveth it of him.

28:19   He that tilleth his land shall have plenty of bread:
      but he that followeth after vain persons
        [empty pursuits] shall have poverty enough.

12:11   He that tilleth his land shall be satisfied
      with bread:
      but he that followeth vain persons is void
      of understanding.

II. **A Good Worker Is Industrious and Faithful**

A.   He Plans and Orders His Tasks

24:27   Prepare thy work without,
      and make it fit for thyself in the field;
      and afterwards build thine house.

B.   He Is Diligent and Conscientious

10:4   He becometh poor that dealeth with a slack hand:
      but the hand of the diligent maketh rich.

21:5   The thoughts of the diligent tend only
      to plenteousness [profit];
      but of every one that is hasty only to want.

C.   He Is Faithful to His Superiors

25:13   As the cold of snow in the time of harvest,
      so is a faithful messenger to them that send him:
      for he refresheth the soul of his masters.

13:17   A wicked messenger falleth into mischief:
      but a faithful ambassador is health.

D.   He Completes His Work on Schedule

10:5   He that gathereth in summer is a wise son:
      but he that sleepeth in harvest is a son that
        causeth shame.

III. **A Good Housewife Works Hard at Home** (From Chapter 31)

    A.   She Is Organized and Skillful

       31:27 She looketh well to the ways of her household,
               and eateth not the bread of idleness.

       31:13 She seeketh wool, and flax,
               and worketh willingly with her hands.
         14 She is like the merchants' ships;
               she bringeth her food from afar.

       31:19 She layeth her hands to the spindle,
               and her hands hold the distaff. . . .
         22 She maketh herself coverings of tapestry;
               her clothing is silk and purple.

    B.   She Works Long Hours

       31:15 She riseth also while it is yet night,
               and giveth meat to her household,
               and a portion to her maidens. . . .
         17 She girdeth her loins with strength,
               and strengtheneth her arms.
         18 She perceiveth that her merchandise is good:
               her candle goeth not out by night.

    C.   She Is Wise in Business and Financial Matters

       31:16 She considereth a field, and buyeth it:
               with the fruit of her hands she planteth
                  a vineyard.

       31:24 She maketh fine linen, and selleth it;
               and delivereth girdles unto the merchant.

    D.   She Is Honored for Her Work

       31:31 Give her of the fruit of her hands;
               and let her own works praise her in the gates.

IV. **A Good Worker Will Be Rewarded**

    A.   He Will Profit From His Labor

       14:23 In all labour there is profit:
               but the talk of the lips tendeth only to penury.

       13:11 Wealth gotten by vanity shall be diminished:
               but he that gathereth by labour shall increase.

B. He Will Advance and Receive Recognition

22:29   Seest thou a man diligent in his business?
          he shall stand before kings;
          he shall not stand before mean men.

12:24   The hand of the diligent shall bear rule:
          but the slothful shall be under tribute.

17:2   A wise servant shall have rule over a son
                that causeth shame,
          and shall have part of the inheritance
                among the brethren.

27:18   Whoso keepeth the fig tree shall eat the fruit thereof:
          so he that waiteth on his master shall be honoured.

C. He Will Enjoy the Fruit of His Labor

10:16   The labour of the righteous tendeth to life:
          the fruit of the wicked to sin.

13:4   The soul of the sluggard desireth, and hath nothing:
          but the soul of the diligent shall be made fat.

LAZINESS

I. Characteristics of a Lazy Person

A. He Has No Ambition

26:14   As the door turneth upon his hinges,
          so doth the slothful upon his bed.

26:15   The slothful hideth his hand in his bosom;
          it grieveth him to bring it again to his mouth.

19:24   A slothful man hideth his hand in his bosom,
          and will not so much as bring it to his mouth again.

B. He Wastes His Resources and Potential

18:9   He also that is slothful in his work
          is brother to him that is a great waster.

12:27   The slothful man roasteth not that which he took
                in hunting:
          but the substance of a diligent man is precious.

24:30   I went by the field of the slothful,
       and by the vineyard of the man void of
          understanding;

31   And, lo, it was all grown over with thorns,
       and nettles had covered the face thereof,
       and the stone wall thereof was broken down.

32   Then I saw, and considered it well:
       I looked upon it, and received instruction.

33   Yet a little sleep, a little slumber,
       a little folding of the hands to sleep:

34   So shall thy poverty come as one that traveleth;
       and thy want as an armed man.

C.   He Makes Excuses for His Inaction

20:4   The sluggard will not plow by reason of the cold;
       therefore shall he beg in harvest, and have nothing.

26:16   The sluggard is wiser in his own conceit
       than seven men that can render a reason.

26:13   The slothful man saith, There is a lion in the way;
       a lion is in the streets.

22:13   The slothful man saith, There is a lion without,
       I shall be slain in the streets.

D.   He Disappoints and Irritates Others

10:26   As vinegar to the teeth, and as smoke to the eyes,
       so is the sluggard to them that send him.

II. The Results of Laziness

A.   The Lazy Person Will Not Achieve His Desires

13:4   The soul of the sluggard desireth, and hath nothing:
       but the soul of the diligent shall be made fat.

21:25   The desire of the slothful killeth him;
       for his hands refuse to labour.

26   He coveteth greedily all the day long:
       but the righteous giveth and spareth not.

B.   He Will Live in Hunger and Poverty

19:15   Slothfulness casteth into a deep sleep;
       and an idle soul shall suffer hunger.

20:13   Love not sleep, lest thou come to poverty;
   open thine eyes, and thou shalt be satisfied
    with bread.

C. His Life Will Be Full of Difficulty

15:19   The way of the slothful man is as an hedge
   of thorns:
   but the way of the righteous is made plain.

D. He Will Remain in an Inferior Position

12:24   The hand of the diligent shall bear rule:
   but the slothful shall be under tribute.

III. Lazy Person! Learn From the Ant!

6:6   Go to the ant, thou sluggard;
   consider her ways, and be wise:

7   Which having no guide, overseer, or ruler,

8   Provideth her meat in the summer,
   and gathereth her food in the harvest.

9   How long wilt thou sleep, O sluggard?
   when wilt thou arise out of thy sleep?

10   Yet a little sleep, a little slumber,
   a little folding of the hands to sleep:

11   So shall thy poverty come as one that travelleth,
   and thy want as an armed man.

BUSINESS PRINCIPLES

I. Be Upright in Business

A. Maintain Your Integrity

11:3   The integrity of the upright shall guide them:
   but the perverseness of transgressors
    shall destroy them.

28:6   Better is the poor that walketh in his uprightness,
   than he that is perverse in his ways,
    though he be rich.

B. Be Honest in All Dealings

16:11   A just weight and balance are the Lord's:
       all the weights of the bag are his work.

11:1   A false balance is abomination to the Lord:
       but a just weight is his delight.

20:23   Divers weights are an abomination unto the Lord;
       and a false balance is not good.

20:10   Divers weights, and divers measures,
       both of them are alike abomination to the Lord.

C. Don't Use the Methods of Ungodly People

3:31   Envy thou not the oppressor,
       and choose none of his ways.

32   For the froward is abomination to the Lord:
       but his secret is with the righteous.

D. Don't Get Involved With Dishonest People

29:24   Whoso is partner with a thief hateth his own soul:
       he heareth cursing, and bewrayeth [tells] it not.

E. Don't Participate in Bribery

   1. Bribes May Facilitate Certain Purposes . . .

17:8   A gift [bribe] is as a precious stone in the eyes of
       him that hath it:
    whithersoever it turneth, it prospereth.

18:16   A man's gift maketh room for him,
       and bringeth him before great men.

21:14   A gift in secret pacifieth anger:
       and a reward [bribe] in the bosom strong wrath.

   2. But They Pervert Behavior and Justice

17:23   A wicked man taketh a gift out of the bosom
       to pervert the ways of judgment.

29:4   The king by judgment establisheth the land:
       but he that receiveth gifts overthroweth it.

II. **Get Good Counsel for Major Decisions**

A. Seek Wise and Upright Counsel

1:5   A wise man will hear, and will increase learning;
and a man of understanding shall attain
unto wise counsels:

20:18   Every purpose is established by counsel:
and with good advice make war.

15:22   Without counsel purposes are disappointed:
but in the multitude of counsellors
they are established.

B. Reject Counsel Contrary to God's Word

19:27   Cease, my son, to hear the instruction
that causeth to err from the words of knowledge.

12:5   The thoughts of the righteous are right:
but the counsels of the wicked are deceit.

III. **Be Careful and Fair in Buying and Selling**

A. Know the Value of What You Buy or Sell

20:14   It is nought, it is nought, saith the buyer:
but when he is gone his way, then he boasteth.

B. Be Considerate and Fair With Customers

11:26   He that withholdeth corn, the people shall curse him:
but blessing shall be upon the head of him
that selleth it.

IV. **Be Careful and Fair as an Employer**

A. Be Careful Whom You Hire or Assign Important Tasks

26:6   He that sendeth a message by the hand of a fool
cutteth off the feet, and drinketh damage.

10:26   As vinegar to the teeth, and as smoke to the eyes,
so is the sluggard to them that send him.

20:6   Most men will proclaim every one his own goodness:
but a faithful man who can find?

B. Be Kind and Consistent With Your Employees

  29:21 He that delicately bringeth up his servant
        from a child
      shall have him become his son at the length.

C. Learn How to Correct Your Employees Effectively

  29:19 A servant will not be corrected by words:
      for though he understand he will not answer.

FINANCIAL PRACTICES

I. Settle Obligations Promptly When Due

  3:27 Withhold not good from them to whom it is due,
      when it is in the power of thine hand to do it.
    28 Say not unto thy neighbour, Go, and come again,
      and tomorrow I will give;
      when thou hast it by thee.

II. Avoid the Problems and Risks of Debt

  22:7 The rich ruleth over the poor,
      and the borrower is servant to the lender.

III. Avoid Using Guarantees

A. Don't Guarantee Another's Debts

  22:26 Be not thou one of them that strike hands,
      or of them that are sureties for debts.
    27 If thou hast nothing to pay,
      why should he take away thy bed from under thee?

  11:15 He that is surety for a stranger shall smart for it:
      and he that hateth suretiship is sure.

  17:18 A man void of understanding striketh hands,
      and becometh surety in the presence of his friend.

B. Extricate Yourself From Existing Guarantees

  6:1 My son, if thou be surety for thy friend,
      if thou hast stricken thy hand with a stranger,
    2 Thou art snared with the words of thy mouth,
      thou art taken with the words of thy mouth.

3   Do this now, my son, and deliver thyself,
       when thou art come into the hand of thy friend;
       go, humble thyself, and make sure thy friend.
4   Give not sleep to thine eyes,
       nor slumber to thine eyelids.
5   Deliver thyself as a roe from the hand of the hunter,
       and as a bird from the hand of the fowler.

C. Require Collateral for a Stranger's Guarantee

20:16   Take his garment that is surety for a stranger:
         and take a pledge of him for a strange woman.

27:13   Take his garment that is surety for a stranger,
         and take a pledge of him for a strange woman.

IV. **Don't Lend at Excessive Interest**

28:8   He that by usury and unjust gain increaseth
         his substance,
         he shall gather it for him that will pity the poor.

Chapter 14

Material Possessions — Servant or Master?

Honor the Lord with thy substance,
and with the firstfruits of all thine increase:
So shall thy barns be filled with plenty,
and thy presses shall burst out with new wine.

(3:9-10)

	Page
The Believer's Possessions	152
Limitations and Dangers of Riches	154
Covetousness and Greed	157
Poverty and the Poor	159
Food and Eating	162

THE BELIEVER'S POSSESSIONS

I. Recognize That All Material Blessings Come From God

10:22   The blessing of the Lord, it maketh rich,
and he addeth no sorrow with it.

II. Obtain Material Things the Right Way

A.   Through Diligent and Honest Work

10:4   He becometh poor that dealeth with a slack hand:
but the hand of the diligent maketh rich.

13:11   Wealth gotten by vanity shall be diminished:
but he that gathereth by labour shall increase.

B.   Through Effective Use of Your Resources

14:4   Where no oxen are, the crib is clean:
but much increase is by the strength of the ox.

C.   Through Wise and Righteous Endeavor

14:24   The crown of the wise is their riches:
but the foolishness of fools is folly.

24:3   Through wisdom is an house builded;
and by understanding it is established:
4   And by knowledge shall the chambers be filled
with all precious and pleasant riches.

8:18   Riches and honour are with me [wisdom];
yea, durable riches and righteousness. . . .
20   I lead in the way of righteousness,
in the midst of the paths of judgment:
21   That I may cause those that love me
to inherit substance;
and I will fill their treasures.

15:6   In the house of the righteous is much treasure:
but in the revenues of the wicked is trouble.

28:10   Whoso causeth the righteous to go astray
in an evil way,
he shall fall himself into his own pit:
but the upright shall have good things in possession.

D. Through Humble Faith in God

22:4   By humility and the fear of the Lord
      are riches, and honour, and life.

III. Honor God With Your Possessions

A. Dedicate Them to God, and Give to Him First

3:9   Honour the Lord with thy substance,
      and with the firstfruits of all thine increase:
10   So shall thy barns be filled with plenty,
      and thy presses shall burst out with new wine.

B. Give Generously to Those in Need

19:17   He that hath pity upon the poor lendeth
      unto the Lord;
      and that which he hath given will he pay
      him again.

28:27   He that giveth unto the poor shall not lack:
      but he that hideth his eyes shall have many a curse.

11:24   There is that scattereth [gives], and yet increaseth;
      and there is that withholdeth more than is meet,
      but it tendeth to poverty.
25   The liberal soul shall be made fat [prosperous]:
      and he that watereth shall be watered also himself.

IV. Take Good Care of Your Possessions

A. Manage Them Diligently

27:23   Be thou diligent to know the state of thy flocks,
      and look well to thy herds.
24   For riches are not for ever:
      and doth the crown endure to every generation?
25   The hay appeareth, and the tender grass
      sheweth itself,
      and herbs of the mountains are gathered.
26   The lambs are for thy clothing,
      and the goats are the price of the field.
27   And thou shalt have goats' milk enough for thy food,
      for the food of thy household,
      and for the maintenance for thy maidens.

B. Conserve Them Wisely

21:20   There is treasure to be desired and oil
in the dwelling of the wise;
but a foolish man spendeth it up.

12:27   The slothful man roasteth not that which he took
in hunting:
but the substance of a diligent man is precious.

C. Preserve Them for Your Posterity

19:14   House and riches are the inheritance of fathers:
and a prudent wife is from the Lord.

13:22   A good man leaveth an inheritance to his
children's children:
and the wealth of the sinner is laid up for the just.

LIMITATIONS AND DANGERS OF RICHES

I. Riches Have Major Limitations

A. They Are Transitory and Easily Lost

23:4   Labour not to be rich:
cease from thine own wisdom.

5   Wilt thou set thine eyes upon that which is not?
for riches certainly make themselves wings;
they fly away as an eagle toward heaven.

27:24   For riches are not for ever:
and doth the crown endure to every generation?

20:21   An inheritance may be gotten hastily
at the beginning;
but the end thereof shall not be blessed.

B. They Cannot Provide True and Lasting Life

11:28   He that trusteth in his riches shall fall:
but the righteous shall flourish as a branch.

C. They Are of No Value at the Judgment

11:4   Riches profit not in the day of wrath:
but righteousness delivereth from death.

II. **Riches Can Harm Your Soul and Your Character**

A. They Can Turn You From God

30:7 Two things have I required of thee;
   deny me them not before I die:

8 Remove far from me vanity and lies:
   give me neither poverty nor riches;
   feed me with food convenient for me:

9 Lest I be full, and deny thee,
   and say, Who is the Lord?
   or lest I be poor, and steal,
   and take the name of my God in vain.

B. They Can Produce Conceit and False Security

18:11 The rich man's wealth is his strong city,
   and as an high wall in his own conceit.

28:11 The rich man is wise in his own conceit;
   but the poor that hath understanding
      searcheth him out.

C. They Can Lead to Inconsiderate Treatment of Others

18:23 The poor useth entreaties;
   but the rich answereth roughly.

III. **Riches May Bring Certain Benefits . . .**

A. Economic Security

10:15 The rich man's wealth is his strong city:
   the destruction of the poor is their poverty.

13:8 The ransom of a man's life are his riches:
   but the poor heareth not rebuke.

B. Independence and Influence

22:7 The rich ruleth over the poor,
   and the borrower is servant to the lender.

C. Many (Supposed) Friends

19:4 Wealth maketh many friends;
   but the poor is separated from his neighbour.

14:20 The poor is hated even of his own neighbour:
   but the rich hath many friends.

IV. **But Other Possessions Are Better Than Wealth**

A. A Right Relationship to God

15:16 Better is little with the fear of the Lord
       than great treasure and trouble therewith.

B. A Righteous Life

16:8 Better is a little with righteousness
       than great revenues without right.

28:6 Better is the poor that walketh in his uprightness,
       than he that is perverse in his ways,
          though he be rich.

C. Godly Wisdom

16:16 How much better is it to get wisdom than gold!
       and to get understanding rather to be chosen
          than silver!

8:10 Receive my instruction, and not silver;
       and knowledge rather than choice gold.

11 For wisdom is better than rubies;
       and all the things that may be desired
          are not to be compared to it.

D. Love and Peace at Home

15:17 Better is a dinner of herbs where love is,
       than a stalled ox and hatred therewith.

17:1 Better is a dry morsel, and quietness therewith,
       than an house full of sacrifices with strife.

E. A Good Reputation

22:1 A good name is rather to be chosen than great riches,
       and loving favour rather than silver and gold.

V. **Riches Obtained Dishonestly Will Be Troublesome**

A. They Cause Discontent and Emptiness

20:17 Bread of deceit is sweet to a man;
       but afterwards his mouth shall be filled with gravel.

21:6 The getting of treasures by a lying tongue
       is a vanity tossed to and fro of them
          that seek death.

10:2 Treasures of wickedness profit nothing:
    but righteousness delivereth from death.

B. They Will Not Last

13:11 Wealth gotten by vanity shall be diminished:
    but he that gathereth by labour shall increase.

22:16 He that oppresseth the poor to increase his riches,
    and he that giveth to the rich,
    shall surely come to want.

28:8 He that by usury and unjust gain increaseth
    his substance,
    he shall gather it for him that will pity the poor.

C. They Require Restitution

6:30 Men do not despise a thief, if he steal
    to satisfy his soul when he is hungry;
31 But if he be found, he shall restore sevenfold;
    he shall give all the substance of his house.

COVETOUSNESS AND GREED

I. People Are Naturally Inclined Toward Covetousness

27:20 Hell and destruction are never full;
    so the eyes of man are never satisfied.

II. Covetousness and Greed Are Self-Destructive

A. They Lead to Wrong-Doing

28:20 A faithful man shall abound with blessings:
    but he that maketh haste to be rich
        shall not be innocent.
21 To have respect of persons is not good:
    for for a piece of bread that man will transgress.
22 He that hasteth to be rich hath an evil eye,
    and considereth not that poverty shall come
        upon him.

B. They Result in Trouble and Death

15:27 He that is greedy of gain troubleth his own house;
    but he that hateth gifts [bribes] shall live.

1:10 My son, if sinners entice thee,
consent thou not.

11 If they say, Come with us, let us lay wait for blood,
let us lurk privily for the innocent
without cause: . . .

13 We shall find all precious substance,
we shall fill our houses with spoil: . . .

18 And they lay wait for their own blood;
they lurk privily for their own lives.

19 So are the ways of every one that is greedy of gain;
which taketh away the life of the owners thereof.

III. Envy of Wrong-Doers Misleads a Believer

A. Their Apparent Prosperity and Success Are Temporary

24:19 Fret not thyself because of evil men,
neither be thou envious at the wicked;

20 For there shall be no reward to the evil man;
the candle of the wicked shall be put out.

B. Their Values and Methods Are Offensive to God

3:31 Envy thou not the oppressor,
and choose none of his ways.

32 For the froward is abomination to the Lord:
but his secret is with the righteous.

C. Their Companionship Subverts Godly Character

24:1 Be not thou envious against evil men,
neither desire to be with them.

2 For their heart studieth destruction,
and their lips talk of mischief.

23:17 Let not thine heart envy sinners:
but be thou in the fear of the Lord all the day long.

IV. Some Pretend to Be Rich; Others, to Be Poor

13:7 There is that maketh himself rich, yet hath nothing:
there is that maketh himself poor, yet hath
great riches.

V. **Victory Over Covetousness Lengthens Life**

28:16   The prince that wanteth understanding
　　　　　　is also a great oppressor:
　　　　　　but he that hateth covetousness shall prolong
　　　　　　his days.

POVERTY AND THE POOR

I. **Avoidable Causes of Poverty**

A. Laziness

  6:9   How long wilt thou sleep, O sluggard?
　　　　　when wilt thou arise out of thy sleep?
  10   Yet a little sleep, a little slumber,
　　　　　a little folding of the hands to sleep:
  11   So shall thy poverty come as one that travelleth,
　　　　　and thy want as an armed man.

20:13   Love not sleep, lest thou come to poverty;
　　　　　open thine eyes, and thou shalt be satisfied
　　　　　　with bread.

13:4   The soul of the sluggard desireth, and hath nothing:
　　　　　but the soul of the diligent shall be made fat.

14:23   In all labour there is profit:
　　　　　but the talk of the lips tendeth only to penury.

B. Love of Pleasure

21:17   He that loveth pleasure shall be a poor man:
　　　　　he that loveth wine and oil shall not be rich.

23:21   For the drunkard and the glutton shall come
　　　　　　to poverty:
　　　　　and drowsiness shall clothe a man with rags.

28:19   He that tilleth his land shall have plenty of bread:
　　　　　but he that followeth after vain persons shall have
　　　　　　poverty enough.

C. Careless Acts and Hasty Decisions

10:4   He becometh poor that dealeth with a slack hand:
　　　　　but the hand of the diligent maketh rich.

21:5   The thoughts of the diligent tend only
                to plenteousness;
            but of every one that is hasty only to want.

D. Schemes to "Get Rich Quick"

28:2   He that hasteth to be rich hath an evil eye,
            and considereth not that poverty shall come
                upon him.

E. Oppressive Greed

22:16   He that oppresseth the poor to increase his riches,
            and he that giveth to the rich,
                shall surely come to want.

11:24   There is that scattereth, and yet increaseth;
            and there is that withholdeth more than is meet,
                but it tendeth to poverty.

F. Rejection of Instruction

13:18   Poverty and shame shall be to him that refuseth
                instruction:
            but he that regardeth reproof shall be honoured.

II. **The Results of Poverty**

A. Economic Subjection

22:7   The rich ruleth over the poor,
            and the borrower is servant to the lender.

18:23   The poor useth entreaties;
            but the rich answereth roughly.

B. Exposure to Injustice and Exploitation

13:23   Much food is in the tillage of the poor:
            but there is that is destroyed for want of judgment.

30:14   There is a generation, whose teeth are as swords,
            and their jaw teeth as knives,
        to devour the poor from off the earth,
            and the needy from among men.

C. A Lack and Loss of Friends

14:20   The poor is hated even of his own neighbour:
            but the rich hath many friends.

19:4   Wealth maketh many friends;
 but the poor is separated from his neighbour.

19:7   All the brethren of the poor do hate him:
 how much more do his friends go far from him?
 he pursueth them with words, yet they are wanting
  to him.

D.   Deprivation and Ruin

10:15   The rich man's wealth is his strong city:
 the destruction of the poor is their poverty.

III. The Innocent Poor and Needy

A.   God Is Their Maker and Defender

22:2   The rich and poor meet together:
 the Lord is the maker of them all.

14:31   He that oppresseth the poor reproacheth his Maker:
 but he that honoureth him hath mercy on the poor.

17:5   Whoso mocketh the poor reproacheth his Maker:
 and he that is glad at calamities shall not
  be unpunished.

22:22   Rob not the poor, because he is poor:
 neither oppress the afflicted in the gate:

 23   For the Lord will plead their cause,
 and spoil the soul of those that spoiled them.

B.   Poverty Is Better Than Unrighteousness

28:6   Better is the poor that walketh in his uprightness,
 than he that is perverse in his ways,
  though he be rich.

19:1   Better is the poor that walketh in his integrity,
 than he that is perverse in his lips, and is a fool.

16:8   Better is a little with righteousness
 than great revenues without right.

IV. The Believer's Response to the Poor

A.   Be Sensitive to Their Plight

29:7   The righteous considereth the cause of the poor:
 but the wicked regardeth not to know it.

21:13   Whoso stoppeth his ears at the cry of the poor,
            he also shall cry himself, but shall not be heard.

B.   Show Them Kindness and Mercy

31:20   She stretcheth out her hand to the poor;
            yea, she reacheth forth her hands to the needy.

14:21   He that despiseth his neighbour sinneth:
            but he that hath mercy on the poor, happy is he.

C.   Give Generously for Their Need

22:9   He that hath a bountiful eye shall be blessed;
            for he giveth of his bread to the poor.

28:27   He that giveth unto the poor shall not lack:
            but he that hideth his eyes shall have many a curse.

19:17   He that hath pity upon the poor lendeth
            unto the Lord;
        and that which he hath given will he
            pay him again.

D.   Defend Them From Injustices

31:9   Open thy mouth, judge righteously,
        and plead the cause of the poor and needy.

FOOD AND EATING

I. Trust God to Provide the Food You Need . . .

10:3   The Lord will not suffer the soul of the righteous
            to famish:
        but he casteth away the substance of the wicked.

13:25   The righteous eateth to the satisfying of his soul:
            but the belly of the wicked shall want.

30:8   Remove far from me vanity and lies:
            give me neither poverty nor riches;
            feed me with food convenient for me:

9   Lest I be full, and deny thee,
            and say, Who is the Lord?
            or lest I be poor, and steal,
            and take the name of my God in vain.

II. **But Also Work to Obtain Your Food**

16:26 He that laboureth laboureth for himself;
for his mouth craveth it of him.

28:19 He that tilleth his land shall have plenty of bread:
but he that followeth after vain persons
[empty pursuits] shall have poverty enough.

19:15 Slothfulness casteth into a deep sleep;
and an idle soul shall suffer hunger.

27:23 Be thou diligent to know the state of thy flocks,
and look well to thy herds. . . .

27 And thou shalt have goats' milk enough for thy food,
for the food of thy household,
and for the maintenance for thy maidens.

31:14 She is like the merchants' ships;
she bringeth her food from afar.

15 She riseth also while it is yet night,
and giveth meat to her household,
and a portion to her maidens.

16 She considereth a field, and buyeth it:
with the fruit of her hands she planteth a vineyard.

III. **Use Self-Control and Discretion in Eating**

A. Eat With Moderation

25:16 Hast thou found honey?
eat so much as is sufficient for thee,
lest thou be filled therewith, and vomit it.

27:7 The full soul loatheth an honeycomb;
but to the hungry soul every bitter thing is sweet.

25:27 It is not good to eat much honey:
so for men to search their own glory is not glory.

B. Don't Eat (i.e., Fellowship) With Sinful People

23:20 Be not among winebibbers;
among riotous eaters of flesh:

21 For the drunkard and the glutton shall come
to poverty:
and drowsiness shall clothe a man with rags.

23:6   Eat thou not the bread of him that hath an evil eye,
   neither desire thou his dainty meats:

7   For as he thinketh in his heart, so is he:
   Eat and drink, saith he to thee;
   but his heart is not with thee.

8   The morsel which thou hast eaten shalt
    thou vomit up,
   and lose thy sweet words.

C. Practice Restraint When Eating With Superiors

23:1   When thou sittest to eat with a ruler,
   consider diligently what is before thee:

2   And put a knife to thy throat,
   if thou be a man given to appetite.

3   Be not desirous of his dainties:
   for they are deceitful meat.

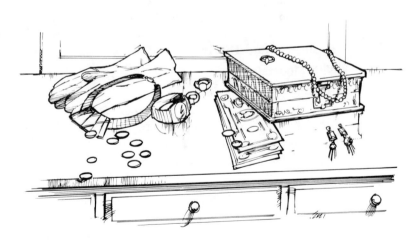

Chapter 15

Sin and Its Curse

*His own iniquities shall take the wicked himself,
and he shall be holden with the cords of his sins.*

(5:22)

	Page
Sin and the Sinner	166
Temptation and Deliverance	169
Strong Drink	171
Immorality Versus Chastity	173
Immorality's Deception and Destruction	176
Shame and Disgrace	179

SIN AND THE SINNER

I. **Man and Sin**

    A. "All Have Sinned and Come Short of the Glory of God" (Rom. 3:23).

      19:3 The foolishness of man perverteth his way:
            and his heart fretteth against the Lord.

      21:8 The way of man is froward and strange:
            but as for the pure, his work is right.

    B. "If We Say That We Have No Sin . . .

      20:9 Who can say, I have made my heart clean,
            I am pure from my sin?

    C. We Deceive Ourselves, and the Truth Is Not in Us" (I John 1:8).

      14:12 There is a way which seemeth right unto a man,
             but the end thereof are the ways of death.

      30:12 There is a generation that are pure in their own eyes,
             and yet is not washed from their filthiness.

    D. "For the Wages of Sin Is Death; . . .

      11:19 As righteousness tendeth to life:
             so he that pursueth evil pursueth it to his
             own death.

      8:36 But he that sinneth against me wrongeth
           his own soul:
           all they that hate me love death.

    E. But the Gift of God Is Eternal Life . . ." (Rom. 6:23).

      8:35 For whoso findeth me findeth life,
           and shall obtain favour of the Lord.

II. **Basic Sins** (Which Lead to Further Sins)

    A. Pride

      21:4 An high look, and a proud heart,
           and the plowing [the lamp] of the wicked, is sin.

28:25   He that is of a proud heart stirreth up strife:
      but he that putteth his trust in the Lord
         shall be made fat.

17:19   He loveth transgression that loveth strife:
      and he that exalteth his gate seeketh destruction.

B. Evil Thoughts

24:8   He that deviseth to do evil
      shall be called a mischievous person.
  9   The thought of foolishness is sin:
      and the scorner is an abomination to men.

6:14   Frowardness is in his heart,
      he deviseth mischief continually; he soweth discord.

14:22   Do they not err that devise evil?
      but mercy and truth shall be to them
         that devise good.

C. Anger and Hatred

29:22   An angry man stirreth up strife,
      and a furious man aboundeth in transgression.

14:21   He that despiseth his neighbour sinneth:
      but he that hath mercy on the poor, happy is he.

D. Covetousness

28:20   A faithful man shall abound with blessings:
      but he that maketh haste to be rich shall not
         be innocent.
  21   To have respect of persons is not good:
      for for a piece of bread that man will transgress.
  22   He that hasteth to be rich hath an evil eye,
      and considereth not that poverty shall come
         upon him.

E. Deceit and Lies

26:23   Burning lips and a wicked heart
      are like a potsherd covered with silver dross.
  24   He that hateth dissembleth [hides it] with his lips,
      and layeth up deceit within him;
  25   When he speaketh fair, believe him not:
      for there are seven abominations in his heart.

III. **The Results of Sin**

  A. Bondage to Sin

     5:22 His own iniquities shall take the wicked himself,
           and he shall be holden with the cords of his sins.

    29:6 In the transgression of an evil man there is a snare:
           but the righteous doth sing and rejoice.

    11:6 The righteousness of the upright shall deliver them:
           but transgressors shall be taken in their own
              naughtiness.

  B. Continuous Trouble

    13:21 Evil pursueth sinners:
           but to the righteous good shall be repayed.

    11:31 Behold, the righteous shall be recompensed
           in the earth:
           much more the wicked and the sinner.

    13:15 Good understanding giveth favour:
           but the way of transgressors is hard.

  C. Frustration and Defeat

    22:8 He that soweth iniquity shall reap vanity:
           and the rod of his anger shall fail.

    13:6 Righteousness keepeth him that is upright
           in the way:
           but wickedness overthroweth the sinner.

    22:12 The eyes of the Lord preserve knowledge,
           and he overthroweth the words of the transgressor.

  D. Shame and Reproach

    13:5 A righteous man hateth lying:
           but a wicked man is loathsome, and cometh
           to shame.

    14:34 Righteousness exalteth a nation:
           but sin is a reproach to any people.

  E. Callous Self-Justification

    28:24 Whoso robbeth his father or his mother,
           and saith, It is no transgression;
           the same is the companion of a destroyer.

30:20 Such is the way of an adulterous woman;
    she eateth, and wipeth her mouth,
    and saith, I have done no wickedness.

F. Condemnation by God

12:2 A good man obtaineth favour of the Lord:
    but a man of wicked devices will he condemn.

10:29 The way of the Lord is strength to the upright:
    but destruction shall be to the workers of iniquity.

IV. **The Believer's Response to Sin**

A. "If We Confess Our Sins . . .

28:13 He that covereth his sins shall not prosper:
    but whoso confesseth and forsaketh them
      shall have mercy.

B. He Is Faithful and Just to Forgive . . .
  and to Cleanse Us . . ." (I John 1:9).

16:6 By mercy and truth iniquity is purged:
    and by the fear of the Lord men depart from evil.

C. "How Shall We, That Are Dead to Sin, . . .

14:27 The fear of the Lord is a fountain of life,
    to depart from the snares of death.

D. Live Any Longer Therein?" (Rom. 6:2).

8:13 The fear of the Lord is to hate evil:
    pride, and arrogancy, and the evil way,
    and the froward mouth, do I hate.

TEMPTATION AND DELIVERANCE

I. **Resist Temptation From Within**

A. The Lust of the Flesh

6:25 Lust not after her beauty in thine heart;
    neither let her take thee with her eyelids.

26 For by means of a whorish woman a man is brought
    to a piece of bread:
    and the adulteress will hunt for the precious life.

23:20   Be not among winebibbers;
    among riotous eaters of flesh:
 21   For the drunkard and the glutton shall come
    to poverty:
    and drowsiness shall clothe a man with rags.

B.   The Lust of the Eyes

27:20   Hell and destruction are never full;
    so the eyes of man are never satisfied.

23:4   Labour not to be rich:
    cease from thine own wisdom.
 5   Wilt thou set thine eyes upon that which is not?
    for riches certainly make themselves wings;
    they fly away as an eagle toward heaven.

C.   The Pride of Life

21:2   Every way of a man is right in his own eyes:
    but the Lord pondereth the hearts.

30:8   Remove far from me vanity and lies:
    give me neither poverty nor riches;
    feed me with food convenient for me:
 9   Lest I be full, and deny thee,
    and say, Who is the Lord?
    or lest I be poor, and steal,
    and take the name of my God in vain.

II. **Resist Temptation From Others** (From Chapter 1)

A.   Promised Excitement

1:10   My son, if sinners entice thee,
    consent thou not.
 11   If they say, Come with us, let us lay wait for blood,
    let us lurk privily for the innocent without cause:
 12   Let us swallow them up alive as the grave;
    and whole, as those that go down into the pit:

B.   Promised Quick Riches

1:13   We shall find all precious substance,
    we shall fill our houses with spoil:

C. Promised Companionship

1:14   Cast in thy lot among us;
let us all have one purse:

III. **Avoid and Overcome Temptation**

A. By Avoiding Sinful People

1:15   My son, walk not thou in the way with them;
refrain thy foot from their path:

16   For their feet run to evil,
and make haste to shed blood.

17   Surely in vain the net is spread
in the sight of any bird.

4:14   Enter not into the path of the wicked,
and go not in the way of evil men.

15   Avoid it, pass not by it,
turn from it, and pass away.

16:29   A violent man enticeth his neighbour,
and leadeth him into the way that is not good.

B. By Heeding God's Word

19:16   He that keepeth the commandment keepeth
his own soul;
but he that despiseth his ways shall die.

6:23   For the commandment is a lamp;
and the law is light;
and reproofs of instruction are the way of life:

24   To keep thee from the evil woman,
from the flattery of the tongue of a strange woman.

STRONG DRINK

I. **Strong Drink Deceives Its Users**

A. It Looks Attractive But Is Deadly

23:31   Look not thou upon the wine when it is red,
when it giveth his colour [sparkles] in the cup,
when it moveth itself aright [goes down smoothly].

32   At the last it biteth like a serpent,
and stingeth like an adder.

B. It Mocks Those Who Are Fooled by It

20:1   Wine is a mocker, strong drink is raging [a brawler]:
and whosoever is deceived thereby is not wise.

II. Strong Drink Affects the Mind

A. It Prevents Clear Thinking and Discernment

31:4   It is not for kings, O Lemuel,
it is not for kings to drink wine;
nor for princes strong drink:

5   Lest they drink, and forget the law,
and pervert the judgment of any of the afflicted.

B. It Generates Perverted Thoughts

23:33   Thine eyes shall behold strange women,
and thine heart shall utter perverse things.

C. It Obscures Impending Disaster

31:6   Give strong drink unto him that is ready to perish,
and wine unto those that be of heavy hearts.

7   Let him drink, and forget his poverty,
and remember his misery no more.

III. Strong Drink Ruins a Life

A. It Enslaves Its Users

23:34   Yea, thou shalt be as he that lieth down in the midst
of the sea,
or as he that lieth upon the top of a mast.

35   They have stricken me, shalt thou say,
and I was not sick:
they have beaten me, and I felt it not:
when shall I awake?
I will seek it yet again.

B. It Leads to Dissipation and Poverty

23:20   Be not among winebibbers;
among riotous eaters of flesh:

21   For the drunkard and the glutton shall come
        to poverty:
      and drowsiness shall clothe a man with rags.

C. It Brings Sorrow and Shame

23:29   Who hath woe? who hath sorrow?
         who hath contentions? who hath babbling?
         who hath wounds without cause?
         who hath redness of eyes?

30   They that tarry long at the wine;
      they that go to seek mixed wine.

IMMORALITY VERSUS CHASTITY

I. Immorality Is Rejection and Defiance of God

2:16   To deliver thee from the strange woman,
         even from the stranger which flattereth
            with her words;

17   Which forsaketh the guide [partner] of her youth,
      and forgetteth the covenant of her God.

30:20   Such is the way of an adulterous woman;
         she eateth, and wipeth her mouth,
         and saith, I have done no wickedness.

II. Immorality Parallels Spiritual Foolishness

9:13   A foolish woman is clamorous:
        she is simple, and knoweth nothing.

14   For she sitteth at the door of her house,
      on a seat in the high places of the city,

15   To call passengers who go right on their ways:

16   Whoso is simple, let him turn in hither:
      and as for him that wanteth understanding,
         she saith to him,

17   Stolen waters are sweet,
      and bread eaten in secret is pleasant.

18   But he knoweth not that the dead are there;
      and that her guests are in the depths of hell.

III. **Immorality Brings Judgment; Chastity Brings Blessing**
   (Chapter 5)

  A. Beware of Immorality's Apparent Attractiveness

    5:1 My son, attend unto my wisdom,
          and bow thine ear to my understanding:

      2 That thou mayest regard discretion,
          and that thy lips may keep knowledge.

      3 For the lips of a strange woman drop
          as an honeycomb,
          and her mouth is smoother than oil:

  B. Recognize Its True Destructive Nature

    5:4 But her end is bitter as wormwood,
          sharp as a twoedged sword.

      5 Her feet go down to death;
          her steps take hold on hell.

      6 Lest thou shouldest ponder the path of life,
          her ways are moveable [unstable], that thou canst
          not know them.

  C. Flee From Its Temptation

    5:7 Hear me now therefore, O ye children,
          and depart not from the words of my mouth.

      8 Remove thy way far from her,
          and come not nigh the door of her house:

  D. Avoid Its Disastrous Consequences

    5:9 Lest thou give thine honour unto others,
          and thy years unto the cruel:

     10 Lest strangers be filled with thy wealth;
          and thy labours be in the house of a stranger;

     11 And thou mourn at the last,
          when thy flesh and thy body are consumed,

     12 And say, How have I hated instruction,
          and my heart despised reproof;

     13 And have not obeyed the voice of my teachers,
          nor inclined mine ear to them that instructed me!

     14 I was almost in all evil [utter ruin]
          in the midst of the congregation and assembly.

E. Enjoy the Blessing of Faithfulness in Marriage

5:15 Drink waters out of thine own cistern,
        and running waters out of thine own well.

16 Let thy fountains be dispersed abroad,
        and rivers of waters in the streets.
            (Or, "Why let . . . ?")

17 Let them be only thine own,
        and not strangers' with thee.

18 Let thy fountain be blessed:
        and rejoice with the wife of thy youth.

19 Let her be as the loving hind and pleasant roe [doe];
        let her breasts satisfy thee at all times;
        and be thou ravished always with her love.

IV. God Observes All Immoral Thoughts and Deeds

5:20 And why wilt thou, my son, be ravished with
            a strange woman,
        and embrace the bosom of a stranger?

21 For the ways of man are before the eyes of the Lord,
        and he pondereth all his goings.

V. Sins of Immorality Lead to Death

5:22 His own iniquities shall take the wicked himself,
        and he shall be holden with the cords of his sins.

23 He shall die without instruction;
        and in the greatness of his folly
            he shall go astray.

VI. God's Word Can Keep You From Immorality

6:20 My son, keep thy father's commandment,
        and forsake not the law of thy mother: . . .

23 For the commandment is a lamp; and the law is light;
        and reproofs of instruction are the way of life:

24 To keep thee from the evil woman,
        from the flattery of the tongue of a strange woman.

IMMORALITY'S DECEPTION AND DESTRUCTION

I. **Guard Against Immorality** (Chapter 7)

    A. Heed the Instruction of Godly Parents

      7:1   My son, keep my words,
            and lay up my commandments with thee.

        2   Keep my commandments, and live;
            and my law as the apple of thine eye.

        3   Bind them upon thy fingers,
            write them upon the table of thine heart.

    B. Overcome Temptation With Godly Wisdom

      7:4   Say unto wisdom, Thou art my sister;
            and call understanding thy kinswoman:

        5   That they may keep thee from the strange woman,
            from the stranger which flattereth with her words.

II. **Beware of Immorality's Points of Attack**

    A. Youthful Naiveté

      7:6   For at the window of my house
            I looked through my casement,

        7   And beheld among the simple ones,
            I discerned among the youths,
            a young man void of understanding,

    B. Intentional Exposure to Temptation

      7:8   Passing through the street near her corner;
            and he went the way to her house,

        9   In the twilight, in the evening,
            in the black and dark night:

    C. Brazen, Unprincipled Women

      7:10 And, behold, there met him a woman
            with the attire of an harlot, and subtil of heart.

       11 (She is loud and stubborn;
            her feet abide not in her house:

       12 Now is she without, now in the streets,
            and lieth in wait at every corner.)

D. Physical Involvement

7:13 So she caught him, and kissed him,
   and with an impudent face said unto him,
 14 I have peace-offerings with me;
   this day have I payed my vows.
 15 Therefore came I forth to meet thee,
   diligently to seek thy face,
    and I have found thee.

E. Enticing Words

7:16 I have decked my bed with coverings of tapestry,
   with carved works, with fine linen of Egypt.
 17 I have perfumed my bed
   with myrrh, aloes, and cinnamon.
 18 Come, let us take our fill of love until the morning:
   let us solace ourselves with loves.
 19 For the goodman [my husband] is not at home,
   he is gone a long journey:
 20 He hath taken a bag of money with him,
   and will come home at the day appointed.
 21 With her much fair speech she caused him to yield,
   with the flattering of her lips she forced him.

F. Overwhelming Lust

7:22 He goeth after her straightway,
   as an ox goeth to the slaughter,
   or as a fool to the correction of the stocks;
 23 Till a dart strike through his liver;
   as a bird hasteth to the snare,
   and knoweth not that it is for his life.

III. **Avoid Immorality's Path**

7:24 Hearken unto me now therefore, O ye children,
   and attend to the words of my mouth.
 25 Let not thine heart decline to her ways,
   go not astray in her paths.
 26 For she hath cast down many wounded:
   yea, many strong men have been slain by her.
 27 Her house is the way to hell,
   going down to the chambers of death.

IV. **Escape Immorality's Destruction**

A. Immorality Cheapens and Humiliates Its Victims

6:25 Lust not after her beauty in thine heart;
     neither let her take thee with her eyelids.
26 For by means of a whorish woman
     a man is brought to a piece of bread:
     and the adulteress will hunt for the precious life.

B. It Squanders Possessions and Position

29:3 Whoso loveth wisdom rejoiceth his father:
     but he that keepeth company with harlots
        spendeth his substance.

31:3 Give not thy strength unto women,
     nor thy ways to that which destroyeth kings.

C. It Traps and Imprisons Its Victims

23:27 For a whore is a deep ditch;
     and a strange woman is a narrow pit.
28 She also lieth in wait as for a prey,
     and increaseth the transgressors among men.

22:14 The mouth of strange women is a deep pit:
     he that is abhorred of the Lord shall fall therein.

D. It Brings Guaranteed Punishment

6:27 Can a man take fire in his bosom,
     and his clothes not be burned?
28 Can one go upon hot coals,
     and his feet not be burned?
29 So he that goeth in to his neighbour's wife;
     whosoever toucheth her shall not be innocent.

E. It Results in Lasting Disgrace

6:30 Men do not despise a thief, if he steal
     to satisfy his soul when he is hungry;
31 But if he be found, he shall restore sevenfold;
     he shall give all the substance of his house.
32 But whoso committeth adultery with a woman
     lacketh understanding:
     he that doeth it destroyeth his own soul.

33   A wound and dishonour shall he get;
    and his reproach shall not be wiped away.

F. It Invites Revenge

6:34 For jealousy is the rage of a man:
    therefore he will not spare in the day of vengeance.
35 He will not regard any ransom;
    neither will he rest content,
    though thou givest many gifts.

G. Its Destruction Is Irreversible

2:18 For her house inclineth unto death,
    and her paths unto the dead.
19 None that go unto her return again,
    neither take they hold of the paths of life.

SHAME AND DISGRACE
(Major Causes of Shame and Disgrace)

I. Foolish Disregard of God

3:35 The wise shall inherit glory:
    but shame shall be the promotion of fools.

II. Sinful Hearts and Lives

13:5 A righteous man hateth lying:
    but a wicked man is loathsome, and cometh
    to shame.

12:8 A man shall be commended according to his wisdom:
    but he that is of a perverse heart shall be despised.

18:3 When the wicked cometh, then cometh
    also contempt,
    and with ignominy [dishonor] reproach.

10:7 The memory of the just is blessed:
    but the name of the wicked shall rot.

14:34 Righteousness exalteth a nation:
    but sin is a reproach to any people.

III. **A Proud and Rebellious Spirit**

   A. Pride

     11:2   When pride cometh, then cometh shame:
           but with the lowly is wisdom.

   B. Rejection of Instruction

     13:18 Poverty and shame shall be to him that refuseth
           instruction:
           but he that regardeth reproof shall be honoured.

   C. Disrespect for Parents

     19:26 He that wasteth [robs] his father, and chaseth away
           his mother,
           is a son that causeth shame, and bringeth reproach.

IV. **Offensive Conduct**

   A. Disgraceful Behavior

     14:35 The king's favour is toward a wise servant:
           but his wrath is against him that causeth shame.

     17:2   A wise servant shall have rule over a son that
           causeth shame,
           and shall have part of the inheritance among
           the brethren.

   B. Uncontrolled Temper

     12:16 A fool's wrath is presently known:
           but a prudent man covereth shame.

V. **Wrong Relationships**

   A. Harmful Friendships

     28:7   Whoso keepeth the law is a wise son:
           but he that is a companion of riotous men shameth
           his father.

   B. Immoral Relationships

     6:32   But whoso committeth adultery with a woman
           lacketh understanding:
           he that doeth it destroyeth his own soul.

33 A wound and dishonour shall he get;
and his reproach shall not be wiped away.

VI. **Failure to Meet Responsibilities**

A. Neglect of Necessary Tasks

10:5 He that gathereth in summer is a wise son:
but he that sleepeth in harvest is a son that
causeth shame.

B. Disregard of Parental Responsibilities

29:15 The rod and reproof give wisdom:
but a child left to himself bringeth his mother
to shame.

VII. **Thoughtless Comments**

A. Hasty Arguments

25:8 Go not forth hastily to strive,
lest thou know not what to do in the end thereof,
when thy neighbour hath put thee to shame.

B. Jumping to Conclusions

18:13 He that answereth a matter before he heareth it,
it is folly and shame unto him.

C. Private Disagreements Made Public

25:9 Debate thy cause with thy neighbour himself;
and discover not a secret to another:

10 Lest he that heareth it put thee to shame,
and thine infamy turn not away.

D. Rebuking Hardened Sinners

9:7 He that reproveth a scorner getteth to himself shame:
and he that rebuketh a wicked man getteth himself
a blot.

Chapter 16

Those Who Do Not Heed God

There is a way that seemeth right unto a man,
but the end thereof are the ways of death.

(16:25)

                                                                    Page

The Natural Man 184

The Naive and Simple 185

The Fool 187

The Scoffer 192

The Wicked 193

THE NATURAL MAN

I. His Basic Condition

A. He Thinks That He Is "Okay"

16:2   All the ways of a man are clean in his own eyes;
         but the Lord weigheth the spirits.

21:2   Every way of a man is right in his own eyes:
         but the Lord pondereth the hearts.

14:12   There is a way which seemeth right unto a man,
         but the end thereof are the ways of death.

B. He Does Not Understand His Spiritual Need

20:24   Man's goings are of the Lord;
         how can a man then understand his own way?

30:12   There is a generation that are pure in their own eyes,
         and yet is not washed from their filthiness.

C. He Is Never Truly Satisfied

27:20   Hell and destruction are never full;
         so the eyes of man are never satisfied.

D. He Habitually Sins

21:8   The way of man is froward and strange:
         but as for the pure, his work is right.

19:3   The foolishness of man perverteth his way:
         and his heart fretteth against the Lord.

E. He Is Unable to Remedy His Condition

20:9   Who can say, I have made my heart clean,
         I am pure from my sin?

II. His Tragic End

A. His Life Will Be Full of Trouble

22:5   Thorns and snares are in the way of the froward:
         he that doth keep his soul shall be far from them.

17:20   He that hath a froward heart findeth no good:
         and he that hath a perverse tongue falleth
              into mischief.

B. His Way Will End in Eternal Death

16:25 There is a way that seemeth right unto a man,
    but the end thereof are the ways of death.

29:18 Where there is no vision [revelation from God],
    the people perish:
but he that keepeth the law, happy is he.

21:16 The man that wandereth out of the way
    of understanding
shall remain in the congregation of the dead.

III. The Believer's Response to the Natural Man

A. Warn Him of His Helpless Condition

24:11 If thou forbear to deliver them that are drawn
    unto death,
and those that are ready to be slain;

12 If thou sayest, Behold, we knew it not;
doth not he that pondereth the heart consider it?
and he that keepeth thy soul, doth not he know it?
and shall not he render to every man according
    to his works?

B. Encourage Him to Turn to God

11:30 The fruit of the righteous is a tree of life;
and he that winneth souls is wise.

THE NAIVE AND SIMPLE

I. His Basic Condition

A. He Lacks Wisdom

8:5 O ye simple, understand wisdom:
and, ye fools, be ye of an understanding heart.

B. He Is Easily Misled

14:15 The simple believeth every word:
but the prudent man looketh well to his going.

9:13 A foolish woman is clamorous:
she is simple, and knoweth nothing. . . .

16   Whoso is simple, let him turn in hither:
 and as for him that wanteth understanding,
  she saith to him,
17   Stolen waters are sweet,
 and bread eaten in secret is pleasant.
18   But he knoweth not that the dead are there;
 and that her guests are in the depths of hell.

C.   He Is Susceptible to Temptation

7:6   For at the window of my house
 I looked through my casement,
7   And beheld among the simple ones,
 I discerned among the youths,
  a young man void of understanding, . . .
10   And, behold, there met him a woman
 with the attire of an harlot, and subtil of heart. . . .
22   He goeth after her straightway,
 as an ox goeth to the slaughter,
  or as a fool to the correction of the stocks;
23   Till a dart strike through his liver;
 as a bird hasteth to the snare,
  and knoweth not that it is for his life.

D.   He Regularly Stumbles Into Trouble

22:3   A prudent man foreseeth the evil [danger],
  and hideth himself:
 but the simple pass on, and are punished.

E.   He Is Content in His Ignorance

1:22   How long, ye simple ones, will ye love simplicity?
 and the scorners delight in their scorning,
 and fools hate knowledge?

II. His Tragic End

A.   He Is Drifting Toward Irreversible Foolishness

14:18   The simple inherit folly:
 but the prudent are crowned with knowledge.

B.   He Faces Eventual Destruction

1:32   For the turning away of the simple shall slay them,
 and the prosperity of fools shall destroy them.

III. **The Believer's Response to the Naive**

    A. Warn Him Through the Example of Punished Sinners

    21:11 When the scorner is punished,
          the simple is made wise:
        and when the wise is instructed,
          he receiveth knowledge.

    19:25 Smite a scorner, and the simple will beware:
        and reprove one that hath understanding,
        and he will understand knowledge.

    B. Teach Him God's Truth

    8:5 O ye simple, understand wisdom:
      and, ye fools, be ye of an understanding heart.
    6 Hear; for I will speak of excellent things;
      and the opening of my lips shall be right things.
    7 For my mouth shall speak truth;
      and wickedness is an abomination to my lips.

    1:1 The proverbs of Solomon the son of David,
      king of Israel; . . .
    4 To give subtilty to the simple,
      to the young man knowledge and discretion.

    C. Show Him the Way of Life

    9:1 Wisdom hath builded her house,
      she hath hewn out her seven pillars: . . .
    4 Whoso is simple, let him turn in hither:
      as for him that wanteth understanding,
        she saith to him, . . .
    6 Forsake the foolish, and live;
      and go in the way of understanding.

THE FOOL
(One Who Acts as If There Is No God)

I. **His Basic Condition**

    A. He Is Self-Reliant and Proud

    28:26 He that trusteth in his own heart is a fool:
        but whoso walketh wisely, he shall be delivered.

12:15   The way of a fool is right in his own eyes:
         but he that hearkeneth unto counsel is wise.

14:3   In the month of the foolish is a rod of pride:
         but the lips of the wise shall preserve them.

B. He Is Void of Wisdom

24:7   Wisdom is too high for a fool:
         he openeth not his mouth in the gate.

17:16   Wherefore is there a price in the hand of a fool
         to get wisdom,
    seeing he hath no heart to it?

18:2   A fool hath no delight in understanding,
         but that his heart may discover itself.

C. He Rejects Godly Instruction

1:7   The fear of the Lord is the beginning of knowledge:
         but fools despise wisdom and instruction.

1:22   How long, ye simple ones, will ye love simplicity?
         and the scorners delight in their scorning,
         and fools hate knowledge?

D. He Is Deceived by His Own Folly

14:8   The wisdom of the prudent is to understand his way:
         but the folly of fools is deceit.

14:24   The crown of the wise is their riches:
         but the foolishness of fools is folly.

15:21   Folly is joy to him that is destitute of wisdom:
         but a man of understanding walketh uprightly.

II. **His Progression as a Fool**

A. Everyone Is Inclined Toward Foolishness From Birth

22:15   Foolishness is bound in the heart of a child;
         but the rod of correction shall drive it
    far from him.

B. His Former Naiveté Led to Confirmed Foolishness

14:18   The simple inherit folly:
         but the prudent are crowned with knowledge.

C. Now He Is Unchangeable

27:22　Though thou shouldest bray [pound] a fool in a mortar
　　　　among wheat with a pestle,
　　　　yet will not his foolishness depart from him.

26:11　As a dog returneth to his vomit,
　　　　so a fool returneth to his folly.

17:10　A reproof entereth more into a wise man
　　　　than an hundred stripes into a fool.

III. **His Tell Tale Conduct**

A. He Practices and Enjoys Sin

13:19　The desire accomplished is sweet to the soul:
　　　　but it is abomination to fools to depart from evil.

10:23　It is as sport to a fool to do mischief:
　　　　but a man of understanding hath wisdom.

14:9　Fools make a mock at sin:
　　　　but among the righteous there is favour.

B. He Lacks Self-Control

12:16　A fool's wrath is presently known:
　　　　but a prudent man covereth shame.

13:16　Every prudent man dealeth with knowledge:
　　　　but a fool layeth open his folly.

14:16　A wise man feareth, and departeth from evil:
　　　　but the fool rageth, and is confident.

27:3　A stone is heavy, and the sand weighty;
　　　　but a fool's wrath is heavier than them both.

C. He Disdains and Grieves His Parents

15:20　A wise son maketh a glad father:
　　　　but a foolish man despiseth his mother.

15:5　A fool despiseth his father's instruction:
　　　　but he that regardeth reproof is prudent.

17:21　He that begetteth a fool doeth it to his sorrow:
　　　　and the father of a fool hath no joy.

D. He Deserves Severe Punishment

19:29   Judgments are prepared for scorners,
and stripes for the back of fools.

26:3   A whip for the horse, a bridle for the ass,
and a rod for the fool's back.

IV. His Tell Tale Speech

A. It Reveals His Foolish Nature

15:2   The tongue of the wise useth knowledge aright:
but the mouth of fools poureth out foolishness.

12:23   A prudent man concealeth knowledge:
but the heart of fools proclaimeth foolishness.

15:14   The heart of him that hath understanding
seeketh knowledge:
but the mouth of fools feedeth on foolishness.

29:11   A fool uttereth all his mind:
but a wise man keepeth it in till afterwards.

B. It Often Is Illogical

26:7   The legs of the lame are not equal:
so is a parable in the mouth of fools.

26:9   As a thorn goeth up into the hand of a drunkard,
so is a parable in the mouth of fools.

C. It Contributes to His Eventual Downfall

18:6   A fool's lips enter into contention,
and his mouth calleth for strokes.

7   A fool's mouth is his destruction,
and his lips are the snare of his soul.

10:14   Wise men lay up knowledge:
but the mouth of the foolish is near destruction.

V. His Tragic End

A. His Life Will End in Failure and Shame

10:8   The wise in heart will receive commandments:
but a prating [babbling] fool shall fall.

10:10   He that winketh with the eye causeth sorrow:
   but a prating fool shall fall.

11:29   He that troubleth his own house shall inherit
    the wind:
   and the fool shall be servant to the wise of heart.

3:35   The wise shall inherit glory:
   but shame shall be the promotion of fools.

B.   He Will Die in His Self-Determined Condition

10:21   The lips of the righteous feed many:
   but fools die for want of wisdom.

1:32   For the turning away of the simple shall slay them,
   and the prosperity of fools shall destroy them.

VI. The Believer's Response to a Fool

A.   Avoid Him

14:7   Go from the presence of a foolish man,
   when thou perceivest not in him the lips of
    knowledge.

17:12   Let a bear robbed of her whelps [cubs] meet a man,
   rather than a fool in his folly.

B.   Don't Rely on Him

26:6   He that sendeth a message by the hand of a fool
   cutteth off the feet, and drinketh damage.

C.   Don't Give Him Recognition

26:1   As snow in summer, and as rain in harvest,
   so honour is not seemly for a fool.

26:8   As he that bindeth a stone in a sling,
   so is he that giveth honour to a fool.

D.   Don't Debate With Him

29:9   If a wise man contendeth with a foolish man,
   whether he rage or laugh, there is no rest.

23:9   Speak not in the ears of a fool:
   for he will despise the wisdom of thy words.

26:4   Answer not a fool according to his folly,
   lest thou also be like unto him.

E. Rebuke Him Only If It Will Do Him Good

26:5   Answer a fool according to his folly,
lest he be wise in his own conceit.

THE SCOFFER
(One Who Mocks Sin and God's Judgment)

I. His Basic Condition

A. He Is Filled With Pride

21:24   Proud and haughty scorner is his name,
who dealeth in proud wrath.

B. He Mocks Truth and Justice

19:28   An ungodly witness scorneth judgment:
and the mouth of the wicked devoureth iniquity.

C. He Enjoys Being Contemptuous

1:22   How long, ye simple ones, will ye love simplicity?
and the scorners delight in their scorning,
and fools hate knowledge?

D. He Has No Wisdom

14:6   A scorner seeketh wisdom, and findeth it not:
but knowledge is easy unto him that understandeth.

E. He Will Not Accept Correction

15:12   A scorner loveth not one that reproveth him:
neither will he go unto the wise.

13:1   A wise son heareth his father's instruction:
but a scorner heareth not rebuke.

F. He Causes Problems for Others

29:8   Scornful men bring a city into a snare:
but wise men turn away wrath.

II. His Tragic End

A. He Will Be Despised by God and Others

3:34   Surely he scorneth the scorners:
but he giveth grace unto the lowly.

24:9   The thought of foolishness is sin:
       and the scorner is an abomination to men.

B. He Will Be Judged Severely

19:29   Judgments are prepared for scorners,
       and stripes for the back of fools.

9:12   If thou be wise, thou shalt be wise for thyself:
       but if thou scornest, thou alone shalt bear it.

C. His Punishment Warns the Naive

21:11   When the scorner is punished, the simple is
       made wise:
       and when the wise is instructed, he receiveth
       knowledge.

19:25   Smite a scorner, and the simple will beware:
       and reprove one that hath understanding,
       and he will understand knowledge.

III. The Believer's Response to a Scoffer

A. Don't Try to Reprove Him

9:7   He that reproveth a scorner getteth to himself shame:
       and he that rebuketh a wicked man getteth himself
       a blot.

8   Reprove not a scorner, lest he hate thee:
       rebuke a wise man, and he will love thee.

B. Get Rid of Him

22:10   Cast out the scorner, and contention shall go out;
       yea, strife and reproach shall cease.

THE WICKED

I. His Basic Condition

A. He Is in Spiritual Darkness

4:19   The way of the wicked is as darkness:
       they know not at what they stumble.

2:12   To deliver thee from the way of the evil man,
       from the man that speaketh froward things;

13 Who leave the paths of uprightness,
    to walk in the ways of darkness;
14 Who rejoice to do evil,
    and delight in the frowardness of the wicked;
15 Whose ways are crooked,
    and they froward in their paths:

B. He Is Proud and Defiant Before God

14:2 He that walketh in his uprightness feareth the Lord:
      but he that is perverse in his ways despiseth him.

21:4 An high look, and a proud heart,
      and the plowing [the lamp] of the wicked, is sin.

22:29 A wicked man hardeneth his face:
       but as for the upright, he directeth his way.

C. He Is Drawn to Evil

21:10 The soul of the wicked desireth evil:
       his neighbour findeth no favour in his eyes.

17:11 An evil man seeketh only rebellion:
       therefore a cruel messenger shall be sent
       against him.

16:27 An ungodly man diggeth up evil:
       and in his lips there is as a burning fire.

17:4 A wicked doer giveth heed to false lips;
      and a liar giveth ear to a naughty tongue.

D. His Whole Being Is Evil

10:20 The tongue of the just is as choice silver:
       the heart of the wicked is little worth.

6:12 A naughty person, a wicked man,
      walketh with a froward mouth.

13 He winketh with his eyes,
    he speaketh [signals] with his feet,
    he teacheth [points] with his fingers;
14 Frowardness is in his heart,
    he deviseth mischief continually;
    he soweth discord.
15 Therefore shall his calamity come suddenly;
    suddenly shall he be broken without remedy.

II. **Evidences of His Wicked Nature**

A. He Uses Perverse and Harmful Speech

15:28 The heart of the righteous studieth to answer:
but the mouth of the wicked poureth out
evil things.

10:32 The lips of the righteous know what is acceptable:
but the mouth of the wicked speaketh frowardness.

10:11 The mouth of a righteous man is a well of life:
but violence covereth the mouth of the wicked.

12:6 The words of the wicked are to lie in wait for blood:
but the mouth of the upright shall deliver them.

B. He Practices Deceit and Malice

11:18 The wicked worketh a deceitful work:
but to him that soweth righteousness shall be
a sure reward.

26:23 Burning lips and a wicked heart
are like a potsherd covered with silver dross.

24 He that hateth dissembleth with his lips,
and layeth up deceit within him;

25 When he speaketh fair, believe him not:
for there are seven abominations in his heart.

26 Whose hatred is covered by deceit,
his wickedness shall be shewed before the
whole congregation.

C. He Hates Upright People

29:10 The bloodthirsty hate the upright:
but the just seek his soul.

29:27 An unjust man is an abomination to the just:
and he that is upright in the way
is abomination to the wicked.

D. He Leads Others Astray

16:29 A violent man enticeth his neighbour,
and leadeth him into the way that is not good.

30 He shutteth his eyes to devise froward things:
moving his lips he bringeth evil to pass.

12:5   The thoughts of the righteous are right:
but the counsels of the wicked are deceit.

III. **His Tragic End**

A. His Life Will Be Full of Trouble

12:21   There shall no evil happen to the just:
but the wicked shall be filled with mischief.

11:8   The righteous is delivered out of trouble,
and the wicked cometh in his stead.

24:16   For a just man falleth seven times,
and riseth up again:
but the wicked shall fall into mischief.

15:6   In the house of the righteous is much treasure:
but in the revenues of the wicked is trouble.

13:25   The righteous eateth to the satisfying of his soul:
but the belly of the wicked shall want.

B. He Will Not Realize His Desires

11:7   When a wicked man dieth, his expectation
shall perish:
and the hope of unjust men perisheth.

10:28   The hope of the righteous shall be gladness:
but the expectation of the wicked shall perish.

10:24   The fear of the wicked, it shall come upon him:
but the desire of the righteous shall be granted.

C. He Will Be Defeated by His Own Wrong-Doing

5:22   His own iniquities shall take the wicked himself,
and he shall be holden with the cords of his sins.

23   He shall die without instruction;
and in the greatness of his folly he shall go astray.

11:5   The righteousness of the perfect shall direct his way:
but the wicked shall fall by his own wickedness.

21:7   The robbery [violence] of the wicked shall
destroy them;
because they refuse to do judgment [justice].

12:13   The wicked is snared by the transgression of his lips:
but the just shall come out of trouble.

14:32 The wicked is driven away in his wickedness:
   but the righteous hath hope in his death.

D. He Will Be Punished for His Sin

11:21 Though hand join in hand [assuredly], the wicked
   shall not be unpunished:
   but the seed of the righteous shall be delivered.

11:31 Behold, the righteous shall be recompensed
   in the earth:
   much more the wicked and the sinner.

11:23 The desire of the righteous is only good:
   but the expectation of the wicked is wrath.

21:18 The wicked shall be a ransom for the righteous,
   and the transgressor for the upright.

E. He Faces Imminent, Premature Death

10:27 The fear of the Lord prolongeth days:
   but the years of the wicked shall be shortened.

2:22 But the wicked shall be cut off from the earth,
   and the transgressors shall be rooted out of it.

12:7 The wicked are overthrown, and are not:
   but the house of the righteous shall stand.

13:9 The light of the righteous rejoiceth:
   but the lamp of the wicked shall be put out.

F. His Life Will End in Shame

13:5 A righteous man hateth lying:
   but a wicked man is loathsome, and cometh
   to shame.

12:8 A man shall be commended according to his wisdom:
   but he that is of a perverse heart shall be despised.

10:7 The memory of the just is blessed:
   but the name of the wicked shall rot.

IV. **God's Response to the Wicked**

A. God Hates Everything About Him

11:20   They that are of a froward heart are abomination
        to the Lord:
    but such as are upright in their way are his delight.

3:32   For the froward is abomination to the Lord:
    but his secret is with the righteous.

15:26   The thoughts of the wicked are an abomination
        to the Lord:
    but the words of the pure are pleasant words.

15:9   The way of the wicked is an abomination
        unto the Lord:
    but he loveth him that followeth after righteousness.

21:27   The sacrifice of the wicked is abomination:
    how much more, when he bringeth it with a
        wicked mind [evil intent]?

15:29   The Lord is far from the wicked:
    but he heareth the prayer of the righteous.

B. God Actively Opposes Him

21:12   The righteous man wisely considereth the house of
        the wicked:
    but God overthroweth the wicked for
        their wickedness.

10:3   The Lord will not suffer the soul of the righteous
        to famish:
    but he casteth away the substance of the wicked.

3:33   The curse of the Lord is in the house of the wicked:
    but he blesseth the habitation of the just.

14:11   The house of the wicked shall be overthrown:
    but the tabernacle of the upright shall flourish.

C. God Will Eventually Condemn Him

12:2   A good man obtaineth favour of the Lord:
    but a man of wicked devices will he condemn.

16:4   The Lord hath made all things for himself:
    yea, even the wicked for the day of evil [disaster].

10:25   As the whirlwind passeth, so is the wicked no more:
and the righteous is an everlasting foundation.

V. **The Believer's Response to the Wicked**

A.   Don't Associate With Him

4:14   Enter not into the path of the wicked,
and go not in the way of evil men.

15   Avoid it, pass not by it,
turn from it, and pass away.

24:1   Be not thou envious against evil men,
neither desire to be with them.

2   For their heart studieth destruction,
and their lips talk of mischief.

B.   Don't Envy or Emulate Him

24:19   Fret not thyself because of evil men,
neither be thou envious at the wicked;

20   For there shall be no reward to the evil man;
the candle of the wicked shall be put out.

3:31   Envy thou not the oppressor,
and choose none of his ways.

32   For the froward is abomination to the Lord:
but his secret is with the righteous.

C.   Don't Try to Correct Him

9:7   He that reproveth a scorner getteth to himself shame:
and he that rebuketh a wicked man getteth himself
a blot.

D.   Don't Excuse His Wrong-Doing

17:15   He that justifieth the wicked,
and he that condemneth the just,
even they both are abomination to the Lord.

18:5   It is not good to accept the person of the wicked,
to overthrow the righteous in judgment.

28:17   A man that doeth violence to the blood of any person
shall flee to the pit;
let no man stay him.

E. Live a Holy Life Before Him

28:4   They that forsake the law praise the wicked:
        but such as keep the law contend with them.

25:26   A righteous man falling down before the wicked
        is as a troubled fountain, and a corrupt spring.

Chapter 17

Lessons From Nature

Go to the ant, thou sluggard;
consider her ways, and be wise.

(6:6)

                                                                    Page

Parallels Between Nature and Personal Traits 202

Parallels Between Nature and Daily Living 205

Parallels Between Nature and Injurious People 208

Examples in Nature of Wisdom and Strength 210

PARALLELS BETWEEN NATURE AND PERSONAL TRAITS

I. Parallels With Desirable Traits

A.   A Righteous Life

1.   Like Bright Sunlight

4:18   But the path of the just is as the shining light,
       that shineth more and more unto the perfect day.

2.   Like a Flourishing Tree

11:28   He that trusteth in his riches shall fall:
        but the righteous shall flourish as a branch.

12:12   The wicked desireth the net [plunder] of evil men:
        but the root of the righteous yieldeth fruit.

B.   Wisdom and Honey

24:13   My son, eat thou honey, because it is good;
        and the honeycomb, which is sweet to thy taste:
14   So shall the knowledge of wisdom be unto thy soul:
        when thou hast found it, then there shall be
        a reward,
        and thy expectation shall not be cut off.

C.   Pure Speech and Clear, Fresh Water

10:11   The mouth of a righteous man is a well of life:
        but violence covereth the mouth of the wicked.

18:4   The words of a man's mouth are as deep waters,
        and the wellspring of wisdom as a flowing brook.

D.   A Cheerful Spirit

1.   Like an On-going Feast

15:15   All the days of the afflicted are evil:
        but he that is of a merry heart hath
        a continual feast.

2.   Like Good Medicine

17:22   A merry heart doeth good like a medicine:
        but a broken spirit drieth the bones.

   E. Faithfulness and Refreshing Snow

     25:13 As the cold of snow in the time of harvest,
            so is a faithful messenger to them that send him:
            for he refresheth the soul of his masters.

   F. Godly Confidence and a Lion

     28:1 The wicked flee when no man pursueth:
          but the righteous are bold as a lion.

   G. A Virtuous Wife and Priceless Jewels

     31:10 Who can find a virtuous woman?
           for her price is far above rubies.

II. **Parallels With Undesirable Traits**

   A. Unfaithfulness

     1. Like a Straying Bird

     27:8 As a bird that wandereth from her nest,
          so is a man that wandereth from his place.

     2. Like Painful Injuries

     25:19 Confidence in an unfaithful man in time of trouble
          is like a broken tooth, and a foot out of joint.

   B. Laziness

     1. Like a Field of Weeds

     24:30 I went by the field of the slothful,
          and by the vineyard of the man void of
            understanding;
       31 And, lo, it was all grown over with thorns,
          and nettles had covered the face thereof,
          and the stone wall thereof was broken down.
       32 Then I saw, and considered it well:
          I looked upon it, and received instruction.

     2. Like a Hedge of Thorns

     15:19 The way of the slothful man is as an hedge
          of thorns:
          but the way of the righteous is made plain.

3. Like Irritating Vinegar and Smoke

10:26   As vinegar to the teeth, and as smoke to the eyes,
so is the sluggard to them that send him.

4. Unlike the Hardworking Ant

6:6   Go to the ant, thou sluggard;
consider her ways, and be wise:

7   Which having no guide,
overseer, or ruler,

8   Provideth her meat in the summer,
and gathereth her food in the harvest.

C. Indiscretion and a Jeweled Pig

11:22   As a jewel of gold in a swine's snout,
so is a fair woman which is without discretion.

III. Parallels With God and His Word

A. God's Testing and the Refining of Silver and Gold

17:3   The fining pot is for silver, and the furnace for gold:
but the Lord trieth the hearts.

B. God's Examination of Character and a Searchlight

20:27   The spirit of man is the candle of the Lord,
searching all the inward parts of the belly.

C. God's Control of Rulers and of Rivers

21:1   The king's heart is in the hand of the Lord,
as the rivers of water:
he turneth it whithersoever he will.

D. God's Word and a Guiding Light

6:23   For the commandment is a lamp; and the law
is light;
and reproofs of instruction are the way of life:

PARALLELS BETWEEN NATURE AND DAILY LIVING

I. Parallels With Personal Relationships

A. A Friend's Influence and an Iron File

27:17 Iron sharpeneth iron;
  so a man sharpeneth the countenance of his friend.

B. A Friend's Counsel and Pleasing Perfume

27:9 Ointment and perfume rejoice the heart:
  so doth the sweetness of a man's friend
   by hearty counsel.

C. A Faithful Spouse and Continually Refreshing Water

5:15 Drink waters out of thine own cistern,
  and running waters out of thine own well. . . .
 18 Let thy fountain be blessed:
  and rejoice with the wife of thy youth.

D. A Pleased Ruler and Needed Rain

16:15 In the light of the king's countenance is life;
  and his favour is as a cloud of the latter rain.

E. A Provoked Ruler and a Lion

20:2 The fear of a king is as the roaring of a lion:
  whoso provoketh him to anger sinneth against his
   own soul.

19:12 The king's wrath is as the roaring of a lion;
  but his favour is as dew upon the grass.

F. A Guarantor and a Trapped Animal

6:1 My son, if thou be surety for thy friend,
  if thou hast stricken thy hand with a stranger,
 2 Thou art snared with the words of thy mouth,
  thou art taken with the words of thy mouth. . . .
 5 Deliver thyself as a roe from the hand of the hunter,
  and as a bird from the hand of the fowler.

II. **Parallels With Inner Thoughts**

    A. Inner Thoughts and Deep Water

      20:5   Counsel in the heart of man is like deep water;
               but a man of understanding will draw it out.

    B. One's Real Self and Reflections in Water

      27:19 As in water face answereth to [reflects the] face,
               so the heart of man to [reflects the] man.

III. **Parallels With Good Words**

    A. Pleasant Words and Honey

      16:24 Pleasant words are as an honeycomb,
               sweet to the soul, and health to the bones.

    B. Appropriate Comments and Crafted Gold

      25:11 A word fitly spoken
               is like apples of gold in pictures of silver.
         12 As an earring of gold, and an ornament of fine gold,
               so is a wise reprover upon an obedient ear.

    C. Good News and Refreshing Drink

      25:25 As cold waters to a thirsty soul,
               so is good news from a far country.

IV. **Parallels With Bad Words**

    A. Cutting Comments and a Sword

      12:18 There is that speaketh like the piercings of a sword:
               but the tongue of the wise is health.

      25:18 A man that beareth false witness against
               his neighbour
               is a maul, and a sword, and a sharp arrow.

    B. Wicked Talk and Scorching Flames

      16:27 An ungodly man diggeth up evil:
               and in his lips there is as a burning fire.

    C. Gossip and Deep Wounds

      18:8   The words of a talebearer are as wounds,
               and they go down into the innermost parts
               of the belly.

D. Backbiting and a Rain Storm

   25:23 The north wind driveth away rain:
   so doth an angry countenance a backbiting tongue.

E. Unjustified Condemnation and a Straying Bird

   26:2 As the bird by wandering, as the swallow by flying,
   so the curse causeless shall not come.

V. **Parallels With Inappropriate Behavior**

A. Meddling and Grabbing a Wild Dog

   26:17 He that passeth by, and meddleth with strife
   belonging not to him,
   is like one that taketh a dog by the ears.

B. Self-Exaltation and Overeating of Honey

   25:27 It is not good to eat much honey:
   so for men to search their own glory is not glory.

C. Boasting and Empty Rain Clouds

   25:14 Whoso boasteth himself of a false gift
   is like clouds and wind without rain.

D. Insensitivity and Exposing One to Cold Weather

   25:20 As he that taketh away a garment in cold weather,
   and as vinegar upon nitre [soda],
   so is he that singeth songs to an heavy heart.

E. Honoring a Fool and Untimely Weather

   26:1 As snow in summer, and as rain in harvest,
   so honour is not seemly [fitting] for a fool.

VI. **Parallels With Temptations and Lusts**

A. Riches and Fleeing Birds

   23:4 Labour not to be rich:
   cease from thine own wisdom.

   5 Wilt thou set thine eyes upon that which is not?
   for riches certainly make themselves wings;
   they fly away as an eagle toward heaven.

B. Sexual Immorality and Fire

  6:27 Can a man take fire in his bosom,
      and his clothes not be burned?

    28 Can one go upon hot coals,
      and his feet not be burned?

    29 So he that goeth in to his neighbour's wife;
      whosoever toucheth her shall not be innocent.

C. Drinking and Poisonous Snakebites

  23:31 Look not thou upon the wine when it is red,
      when it giveth his colour in the cup,
      when it moveth itself aright.

    32 At the last it biteth like a serpent,
      and stingeth like an adder.

PARALLELS BETWEEN NATURE AND INJURIOUS PEOPLE

I. Parallels With People Who Trouble Others

A. A Contentious Person and Kindling a Fire

  26:21 As coals are to burning coals, and wood to fire;
      so is a contentious man to kindle strife.

B. A Contentious Wife and a Leaky Roof

  27:15 A continual dropping in a very rainy day
      and a contentious woman are alike.

    16 Whosoever hideth her hideth the wind,
      and the ointment of his right hand, which
        bewrayeth itself [grasps oil with his hand].

C. An Angry Person and Churning Butter

  30:33 Surely the churning of milk bringeth forth butter,
      and the wringing of the nose bringeth forth blood:
      so the forcing of wrath bringeth forth strife.

D. A Gossip and Stoking a Fire

  26:20 Where no wood is, there the fire goeth out:
      so where there is no talebearer, the strife ceaseth.

E. An Oppressor and a Severe Storm

   28:3   A poor man that oppresseth the poor
               is like a sweeping rain which leaveth no food.

F. A Wicked Ruler and Fierce Animals

   28:15 As a roaring lion, and a ranging bear;
              so is a wicked ruler over the poor people.

II. **Parallels With People Who Mislead Others**

A. A Hypocrite and Silver-Plated Clay

   26:23 Burning lips and a wicked heart
              are like a potsherd covered with silver dross.

B. A Sinning Believer and Polluted Water

   25:26 A righteous man falling down before the wicked
              is as a troubled fountain, and a corrupt spring.

C. An Adulteress

   1. Like a Deep Pit

   23:27 For a whore is a deep ditch;
              and a strange woman is a narrow pit.

   2. Like a Slaughterer

   7:22 He goeth after her straightway,
              as an ox goeth to the slaughter,
              or as a fool to the correction of the stocks;
    23 Till a dart strike through his liver;
              as a bird hasteth to the snare,
              and knoweth not that it is for his life.

   3. Like Bitter Herbs (Coated With Honey)

   5:3 For the lips of a strange woman drop
              as an honeycomb,
              and her mouth is smoother than oil:
    4 But her end is bitter as wormwood,
              sharp as a twoedged sword.

III. **Parallels With People Who Oppose God**

A. A Fool

1. Like a Dog and Its Vomit

26:11   As a dog returneth to his vomit,
   so a fool returneth to his folly.

2. Like a Raging Mother Bear

17:12   Let a bear robbed of her whelps meet a man,
   rather than a fool in his folly.

3. Like a Stubborn, Unresponsive Donkey

26:3   A whip for the horse, a bridle for the ass,
   and a rod for the fool's back.

4. Like Lame, Unstable Legs

26:7   The legs of the lame are not equal:
   so is a parable in the mouth of fools.

5. Like a Heavy Burden

27:3   A stone is heavy, and the sand weighty;
   but a fool's wrath is heavier than them both.

B. A Wicked Person

1. Like a Strong, Brief Whirlwind

10:25   As the whirlwind passeth, so is the wicked no more:
   but the righteous is an everlasting foundation.

2. Like Impenetrable Darkness

4:19   The way of the wicked is as darkness:
   they know not at what they stumble.

EXAMPLES IN NATURE OF WISDOM AND STRENGTH
(From Chapter 30)

I. **Examples of Wisdom**

A. Small Creatures Assure Their Survival

30:24   There be four things which are little upon the earth,
   but they are exceeding wise:

B. Ants Prepare for Winter

30:25 The ants are a people not strong,
   yet they prepare their meat in the summer;

C. Badgers Find a Safe Home

30:26 The conies [badgers] are but a feeble folk,
   yet make they their houses in the rocks;

D. Locusts Work Together as a Group

30:27 The locusts have no king,
   yet go they forth all of them by bands;

E. Spiders Adapt to Their Surroundings

30:28 The spider taketh hold with her hands,
   and is in kings' palaces.

II. Examples of Strength and Dignity

30:29 There be three things which go well,
   yea, four are comely in going:
30 A lion which is strongest among beasts,
   and turneth not away for any;
31 A greyhound; an he goat also;
   and a king, against whom there is no rising up.

III. Examples of Skill and Grace

30:18 There be three things which are too
    wonderful for me,
   yea, four which I know not:
19 The way of an eagle in the air;
   the way of a serpent upon a rock;
   the way of a ship in the midst of the sea;
   and the way of a man with a maid.

IV. Examples of Unquenchable Thirst

30:15 The horseleach hath two daughters, crying,
    Give, give.
   There are three things that are never satisfied,
   yea, four things say not, It is enough.

16   The grave; and the barren womb;
     the earth that is not filled with water;
     and the fire that saith not, It is enough.

V. Examples of God's Omnipotence

30:4   Who hath ascended up into heaven, or descended?
       who hath gathered the wind in his fists?
       who hath bound the waters in a garment?
       who hath established all the ends of the earth?
       what is his name, and what is his son's name,
          if thou canst tell?

Chapter 18

Summary and Conclusion

*He that followeth after righteousness and mercy
findeth life, righteousness, and honour.*

(21:21)

	Page
The Overall Message of Proverbs	214
Desires and Goals	216
Finding God's Will	220

THE OVERALL MESSAGE OF PROVERBS
(As Crystallized in Key Verses)

I. **Only With God's Direction Can Life Be Worthwhile**

    A. You Cannot Successfully Direct Your Own Life

      20:24 Man's goings are of the Lord;
             how can a man then understand his own way?

      14:12 There is a way which seemeth right unto a man,
             but the end thereof are the ways of death.

      28:26 He that trusteth in his own heart is a fool:
             but whoso walketh wisely, he shall be delivered.

    B. Wisdom for Successful Living Comes From God Alone

      9:10 The fear of the Lord is the beginning of wisdom:
             and the knowledge of the holy is understanding.

      1:7 The fear of the Lord is the beginning of knowledge:
             but fools despise wisdom and instruction.

      2:6 For the Lord giveth wisdom:
             out of his mouth cometh knowledge
             and understanding.

    C. Trust God, Therefore, to Direct Your Life

      3:5 Trust in the Lord with all thine heart;
             and lean not unto thine own understanding.
      6 In all thy ways acknowledge him,
             and he shall direct thy paths.
      7 Be not wise in thine own eyes:
             fear the Lord, and depart from evil.

II. **Follow God's Prescription for a Successful Life**

    A. Regarding God — Serve the Lord in Righteousness

      21:3 To do justice and judgment
             is more acceptable to the Lord than sacrifice.

      15:8 The sacrifice of the wicked is an abomination
             to the Lord:
             but the prayer of the upright is his delight.

11:30 The fruit of the righteous is a tree of life;
　　　　and he that winneth souls is wise.

B. Regarding Yourself — Practice Discipline in Every Area
　　of Life

4:23 Keep thy heart with all diligence;
　　　　for out of it are the issues of life.

24 Put away from thee a froward mouth,
　　　and perverse lips put far from thee.

25 Let thine eyes look right on,
　　　and let thine eyelids look straight before thee.

26 Ponder the path of thy feet,
　　　and let all thy ways be established.

27 Turn not to the right hand nor to the left:
　　　remove thy foot from evil.

C. Regarding Your Family — Encourage One Another
　　in Love

23:26 My son, give me thine heart,
　　　　and let thine eyes observe my ways.

22:6 Train up a child in the way he should go:
　　　　and when he is old, he will not depart from it.

14:1 Every wise woman buildeth her house:
　　　　but the foolish plucketh it down with her hands.

31:28 Her children arise up, and call her blessed;
　　　　her husband also, and he praiseth her.

D. Regarding Others — Cultivate Healthy and Constructive
　　Relationships

13:20 He that walketh with wise men shall be wise:
　　　　but a companion of fools shall be destroyed.

17:17 A friend loveth at all times,
　　　　and a brother is born for adversity.

27:17 Iron sharpeneth iron;
　　　　so a man sharpeneth the countenance of his friend.

E. Regarding Things — Use Your Possessions in Ways
　　That Honor God

3:9 Honour the Lord with thy substance,
　　　and with the firstfruits of all thine increase:

    10   So shall thy barns be filled with plenty,
          and thy presses shall burst out with new wine.

19:17   He that hath pity upon the poor lendeth
          unto the Lord;
       and that which he hath given will he pay
          him again.

III. God Rewards Those Who Trust and Obey Him

A. With Genuine Happiness

16:20   He that handleth a matter wisely shall find good:
       and whoso trusteth in the Lord, happy is he.

29:18   Where there is no vision, the people perish:
       but he that keepeth the law, happy is he.

B. With an Abundant, Satisfying Life

19:23   The fear of the Lord tendeth to life:
       and he that hath it shall abide satisfied;
       he shall not be visited with evil.

21:21   He that followeth after righteousness and mercy
       findeth life, righteousness, and honour.

C. With Everlasting Life

15:24   The way of life is above to the wise,
       that he may depart from hell beneath.

14:32   The wicked is driven away in his wickedness:
       but the righteous hath hope in his death.

10:25   As the whirlwind passeth, so is the wicked no more:
       but the righteous is an everlasting foundation.

DESIRES AND GOALS

I. Achieve Basic Human Desires — As By-Products of Spiritual Goals (From Chapter 3)

A. Happiness and Contentment (Seek Godly Wisdom)

3:13   Happy is the man that findeth wisdom,
      and the man that getteth understanding. . . .

15   She is more precious than rubies:
    and all the things thou canst desire
       are not to be compared unto her. . . .
17   Her ways are ways of pleasantness,
    and all her paths are peace.
18   She is a tree of life to them that lay hold upon her:
    and happy is every one that retaineth her.

B.   Approval and Acceptance (Develop Godly Character)

  3:3   Let not mercy and truth forsake thee:
      bind them about thy neck;
      write them upon the table of thine heart:
  4   So shalt thou find favour and good understanding
    in the sight of God and man.

C.   Success (Follow God's Way, Not Man's)

  3:31   Envy thou not the oppressor,
      and choose none of his ways.
  32   For the froward is abomination to the Lord:
    but his secret is with the righteous.
  33   The curse of the Lord is in the house of the wicked:
    but he blesseth the habitation of the just.

D.   Prosperity (Give Generously to God)

  3:9   Honour the Lord with thy substance,
      and with the firstfruits of all thine increase:
  10   So shall thy barns be filled with plenty,
    and thy presses shall burst out with new wine.

E.   Security (Trust in God)

  3:23   Then shalt thou walk in thy way safely,
      and thy foot shall not stumble.
  24   When thou liest down, thou shalt not be afraid:
    yea, thou shalt lie down, and thy sleep
      shall be sweet.
  25   Be not afraid of sudden fear,
    neither of the desolation [attack] of the wicked,
      when it cometh.
  26   For the Lord shall be thy confidence,
    and shall keep thy foot from being taken.

F. Health and Long Life (Revere and Obey God)

3:1   My son, forget not my law;
           but let thine heart keep my commandments:

2   For length of days, and long life,
           and peace, shall they add to thee.

3:7   Be not wise in thine own eyes:
           fear the Lord, and depart from evil.

8   It shall be health to thy navel,
           and marrow to thy bones.

II. Select and Pursue the Best Goals

A. Knowing God Intimately

2:3   Yea, if thou criest after knowledge,
           and liftest up thy voice for understanding;

4   If thou seekest her as silver,
           and searchest for her as for hid treasures;

5   Then shalt thou understand the fear of the Lord,
           and find the knowledge of God.

B. Learning and Sharing God's Word

22:20   Have not I written to thee excellent things
            in counsels and knowledge,

21   That I might make thee know the certainty of the
            words of truth;
            that thou mightest answer the words of truth
            to them that send unto thee?

C. Living a Pure and Upright Life

11:23   The desire of the righteous is only good:
            but the expectation of the wicked is wrath.

11:27   He that diligently seeketh good procureth favour:
            but he that seeketh mischief, it shall come
            unto him.

22:1   A good name is rather to be chosen than great riches,
            and loving favour rather than silver and gold.

D. Serving God and Others

11:30   The fruit of the righteous is a tree of life;
            and he that winneth souls is wise.

10:21   The lips of the righteous feed many:
        but fools die for want of wisdom.

31:20   She stretcheth out her hand to the poor;
        yea, she reacheth forth her hands to the needy.

III. **Reject Wrong Desires and Goals**

A.   Pleasure and Self-Gratification

21:17   He that loveth pleasure shall be a poor man:
        he that loveth wine and oil shall not be rich.

23:20   Be not among winebibbers;
        among riotous eaters of flesh:
  21   For the drunkard and the glutton shall come
            to poverty:
        and drowsiness shall clothe a man with rags.

18:2   A fool hath no delight in understanding,
        but that his heart may discover itself.

B.   Materialism

23:4   Labour not to be rich:
        cease from thine own wisdom.
  5   Wilt thou set thine eyes upon that which is not?
        for riches certainly make themselves wings;
        they fly away as an eagle toward heaven.

15:27   He that is greedy of gain troubleth his own house;
        but he that hateth gifts shall live.

C.   Self-Exaltation

25:27   It is not good to eat much honey:
        so for men to search their own glory is not glory.

17:19   He loveth transgression that loveth strife:
        and he that exalteth his gate seeketh destruction.

D.   Companionship With Ungodly People

24:1   Be not thou envious against evil men,
        neither desire to be with them.
  2   For their heart studieth destruction,
        and their lips talk of mischief.

28:19   He that tilleth his land shall have plenty of bread:
         but he that followeth after vain persons
            shall have poverty enough.

   E.   Immoral Lust

      6:25   Lust not after her beauty in thine heart;
              neither let her take thee with her eyelids.
      26   For by means of a whorish woman
            a man is brought to a piece of bread:
            and the adulteress will hunt for the precious life.

IV. **Work to Achieve Your Goals**

   A.   Achievement Requires Persistence and Hard Work

      13:4   The soul of the sluggard desireth and hath nothing:
              but the soul of the diligent shall be made fat.

      21:25   The desire of the slothful killeth him;
               for his hands refuse to labour.

   B.   Achievement Brings Satisfaction and Blessing

      13:19   The desire accomplished is sweet to the soul:
               but it is abomination to fools to depart from evil.

      13:12   Hope deferred maketh the heart sick:
               but when the desire cometh, it is a tree of life.

FINDING GOD'S WILL

I. **Recognize That God Has a Purpose and Plan for You**

      20:24   Man's goings are of the Lord;
               how can a man then understand his own way?

      16:4   The Lord hath made all things for himself:
              yea, even the wicked for the day of evil.

II. **Submit Your Will and Your Life to God**

      3:5   Trust in the Lord with all thine heart;
             and lean not unto thine own understanding.
      6   In all thy ways acknowledge him,
           and he shall direct thy paths.

16:3   Commit thy works unto the Lord,
        and thy thoughts shall be established.

III. Confess and Forsake All Known Sin

28:13   He that covereth his sins shall not prosper:
        but whoso confesseth and forsaketh them
           shall have mercy.

16:6   By mercy and truth iniquity is purged:
        and by the fear of the Lord men depart from evil.

IV. Trust God to Reveal His Will to You

28:5   Evil men understand not judgment:
        but they that seek the Lord understand all things.

2:6   For the Lord giveth wisdom:
        out of his mouth cometh knowledge and
           understanding. . . .

9   Then shalt thou understand righteousness,
        and judgment, and equity;
        yea, every good path.

V. Seek God's Direction Through Prayer

15:29   The Lord is far from the wicked:
        but he heareth the prayer of the righteous.

15:8   The sacrifice of the wicked is an abomination
        to the Lord:
        but the prayer of the upright is his delight.

VI. Obtain Guidance From God's Word

6:20   My son, keep thy father's commandment,
        and forsake not the law of thy mother:

21   Bind them continually upon thine heart,
        and tie them about thy neck.

22   When thou goest, it shall lead thee;
        when thou sleepest, it shall keep thee;
        and when thou awakest, it shall talk with thee.

23   For the commandment is a lamp; and the law
        is light;
        and reproofs of instruction are the way of life:

VII. **Expect God to Work Through You**

16:1   The preparations of the heart in man,
and the answer of the tongue,
is from the Lord.

16:9   A man's heart deviseth his way:
but the Lord directeth his steps.

VIII. **Believe God Will Overcome All Obstacles to His Will**

21:30   There is no wisdom nor understanding nor counsel
against the Lord.

19:21   There are many devices in a man's heart;
nevertheless the counsel of the Lord,
that shall stand.

IX. **Anticipate God's Blessing on Your Life**

10:28   The hope of the righteous shall be gladness:
but the expectation of the wicked shall perish.

10:24   The fear of the wicked, it shall come upon him:
but the desire of the righteous shall be granted.

Subject Index

Principal references appear in bold type.

abilities — 12, 53, 58, 62-63, 136
abominations — 7, **15-17**, 74, 79, 102, 135, 167, 189, 193, 198
achievement — 64, **143-144**, 220
adultery — 6, 33, 88, 108, 120, 122, **173-179**, 209
adversity — 43, **47-48**, 104, 109
advice — 2, **65-67**, 127-128, 137
alcohol — 88, 135, **171-173**
anger — **90-91**, 111, 130, 167, 208
approval — 40, 42, 46, 95, 144, 217
arguments — 98, **110-112**, 121, 134, 181, 191, 208
authors — **8-9**, 124, 126

balance (scales) — **16**, 147
blessings — 5, 18, 26-27, 41-42, **45-46**, 53-54, 119, 152, 222
boasting — **97**, 148, 207
borrowing — **149-150**
bribery — 87, **147**, 157
brothers — 104, 108, 112, 131-132, 161
business — 143, **146-150**, 153

care/caution — **78-80**, 97, 118, 139, 148
carelessness — **80**, 88, 159-160
chastening — 7, 67, **69-70**, 104, **125-126**
chastity — 104, 108, 120, **175**
cheerfulness — 84, 89, 202
children — 46, 48, 69, 83, 89, 104, 120, **124-128**, 174, 188
citizens — 135, **138-139**
conceit — 52, **74-76**, 155
confession — 19, **169**, 221
confidence — 19, 42, **47-48**, 88, 109, 132, 203
correction — 7, 32, **67-70**, 125, 149
counsel — 2, **66-67**, 130, 137, 148

covetousness — 3, **157-159,** 167
creation — **12,** 59, 210-212
criticism — 97, 105, 207

death — 6, 15, **30-33,** 52, 100, 166, 175, 185, 191, 197
deceit — 90, **98-99,** 101-102, 134, 167, 195
descendants — 46, 48, **120,** 154
desires — 22, 46, 86-87, 145, 196, **216-220**
diligence — 78, 114-115, 123, **142-144,** 152-153
discipline — 19, 40, 83, **125-126**
discretion — 2, 11, 51, 70, 96-97, 110, 139, 163-164
disgrace — 121, 128, 178, **179-181**
dishonesty — 16, 87, 147, **156-157**
disrespect — **128,** 180, 189
distress — 4, **47,** 87
drunkenness — 88, 130, **171-173**

eating — 45, 53, 130, 139, 142, **162-164**
emotions — 26, 53, 63, **82-91,** 94-95, 126
employees/employers — 142, 148-149
enemies — 19-20, 70, **105,** 110
envy — 27, 30, 42, 131, **158,** 199, 219

faith — 22, **40-42,** 44, 62, 82, **220-222**
faithfulness — 77, 86, **107-109,** 115, 131-132, 142, 203
fear — 4, **47,** 85
fear of the Lord — 2, 5, **26-28,** 56, 77, 113, 124, 127
finances — 143, **149-150**
flattery — **101,** 134, 177
food — 45, 104, 123, 142-144, 153, **162-164**
fools/foolishness — 2-4, 32, 52, 57, 70, 112, 173, **187-192,** 210
forgiveness — 19, 105, 169
friends — 70, 83, 100, 104, 108-109, **130-133,** 155, 161, 205

generosity — 20, **106-107,** 133, 153, 162
gluttony — 130, 159, **163-164**
goals — 5, **38-42,** **216-220**

God — 5-6, **12-21**, 38-42, 50, 59, 72-74, 76-77, 98, 198, 204, 212
God's will — 18, 87, 95, 135, **220-222**
God's Word — 7-8, **21-23**, 38, 87, 171, 175, 204, 218, 221
gossip — 89, **100-101**, 111, 206, 208
grandparents — 120
grave — 3, **30**, 87
greed — 3, 87, **157-159**, 160
grief — 66, **87-89**, 126, 174
guarantees — 88, 133, **149-150**, 205

happiness — 21, 26, 41, 45, 53, **82-84**, 106, 126, 216-217
haste — **80**, 157, 160, 181
hatred — **90-91**, 111, 167, 195
health — 26, 29, 45, 84, 86, 94, 128, 218
heart — 13, 17-18, 29-30, **72-80**, 89, 94
hell (grave) — 18, **30**, 125, 177
home/house — 46, 48, 54, **118-128**
honesty — 16, **147**
honor — 46, 53-54, 78, **113-115**, 120, 122, 124
hope — 31, 45, 82, 86, 222
humility — 40, **76-78**, 113, 139
hunger — 19, 45, 142, **144-146**, 162-163
husbands — **119-120**
hypocrisy — **101-102**, 132, 158, 164, 167, 195, 209

immorality — 6, 17, 33, 88, 101, 131, **173-179**, 208
impartiality — **137**, 157
inheritance — 120, 144, 154
instruction — 2, 7, 15, 22-23, 62-70, 124-128, 146
integrity — **43-44**, 107-109, 122-123, 136-138, 146-147

jealousy — 42, 179
joy — 45, **82-84**, 86, 94-95, 104-105, 126, 138
justice — 3, **16-18**, 99, 137-138, 147, 162

kindness — 20, 82, **104-106**, 114, 123, 162
kings/rulers — 13, 58, **135-139**, 205
knowledge — 2, 5, 17-18, 22, 26, **62-70**, 79, 94, 127

labor — 28, 97, **142-144**, 152, 163
laughter — 89
laziness — **144-146**, 159, 203-204
lending/loans — **149-150**, 155, 157, 160
liars/lies — 17, 90, **98-99**, 167
life — 15, 22-23, 26-27, **28-30**, 43-44, 214-216
love — **104-105**, 118, 120, 124-125, 156, 215
lust — 169-170, **173-179**, 220

marriage — 83, 104, 108, **118-119**, **122-124**, 205
materialism — **154-159**, 219
meddling — 27, 101, 110, 112, 130, 207
men — **119-120**
money — 3, 146-150, **152-162**

naive/naiveté — 2-4, 56-57, 70, **185-187**, 193
nature — 12, **202-212**
neighbors — **133-134**

obedience — 5, 21, 29, **38-40**, 82, 85, 138
objectives — **40-42**, 66, **216-220**
orphans — 20

parents — 2, 65, 120, **124-128**, 181, 189
patience — 80, 95, 110
peace — 23, 26, 42, **85-86**, 95, **110-112**, 128, 133-134
persuasion — 95, 110
pleasure — 15-16, 63, 95
pleasure-seeking — 3, 130, 142, 159, **219**
poor/poverty — 20, 137, 145-146, **159-162**
possessions — 40, 113, **152-164**
praise — **76**, 120, 124
prayer — **16**, 19, 21, 221
pride — 16, **74-76**, 111, 128, 166, 170, 187
priorities — **38-39**, 142, 156, **216-220**
profit — 97, **142-144**
prosperity — 45, 54, 107, 119, 217

protection — 19-20, 23, 41-44, **47-48**, 54-55, 63, 119, 125
proverbs — 2, 8-9, 51
prudence — 51, 58, **78-80**
punishment — 4, **67-70**, 90, 128, 137-138, 178, 190, 197

reaping — 4, **34-35**, 193-200
rebellion — 75, **128**, 180
reproof — 7, **67-70**, 115
reputation — 46, 122, 124, 156
resources — 144-145, **152-154**
respect — 53, 95, **113-115**, 128, 138
revenge — 20, 47, **105**, 134, 179
riches — 27, 33, 45, 59, **152-159**, 170
righteousness — 7, **15-16**, 28, 38-39, 50, 58, 113, 138, 152, 202
rod (spanking) — 69, **125**
rulers/leaders — 13, 30, 83, 89, **135-139**, 205

safety/security — 4, 5, 19, 41-42, **47-48**, 119, 155, 217
salvation — **14-15**, 32, 44, 57-60, 94, 166, 216
satisfaction — 53, 63, **85-87**, 95, 162, 175
scoffers — 70, 112, **192-193**
self-control — 29-30, 39, **78-80**, 90-91, 96-98, 110-112, 163, 189
self-righteousness — 52, 128, 168-170, **184-185**, **187-191**
selfishness — **106-107**, 148, 154-160, 219
servant/service — 42, 114-115, 136-137, **142-144**, 180
separation — **6**, 27, 38-39, 42, 171, 191, 199
shame — 75, 80, 121, 128, 168, 173, **179-181**, 197
simple (naive) — 2, 56-57, **185-187**, 193
sin/sinners — 3, 32, 35, 131, 135, **166-179**, 193-200
slander — 99
sleep — 23, 41, 47, 142, 144-146, 150
slothfulness/sluggards — 80, **144-146**, 159, 203
speech — 30, **94-102**, 110-112, 190, 202
spirit — 84, 86, **89**, 91, 109
sorrow — **87-89**, 126, 173
sovereignty — **12-13**, 41, 73, 222
sowing — 4, **34-35**, 193-200

Party Mallou 736-7210

stealing — **3**, 33, 131, 147, 157
strength — 43, 53, 62, 143, 211
strife — 90, 100, **110-112,**123
strong drink — 88, 135, **171-173**, 208
success — 45, 66, 118-119, 217
surety — 88, 132-133, **149-150**

teaching/training — 7, 22, **65,** 69-70, 124-128
temptation — 3, 6, 33, **169-171,** 174, 176-177, 186, 207-208
thoughts — 14, 16, **72-74**, 172, 206
tolerance — 110
tongue — 30, **94-102**
trust — 22, 40, 44, 88, 122, 162, 214, **220-222**
truth — 16, 23, **98-99,** 114

vanity — **74-76,** 99, 142, 156
vengeance — 20, 47, **105**, 134, 179
violence — 3, **33,** 128

wealth — 27, 33, 45, 59, 99, **152-159**
wickedness — 6, 15-17, 31-35, 73, 167, **193-200**
widows — 20, 119
wisdom — 2-6, 12-15, 26, 29, 38, 41, **50-60,** 85, 94, 113, 127, 136, 152, 210-211
witnessing — 8, 30, **44,** 94, 108, 185, 187
wives — 83, 104, 119-120, **122-124,** 143, 203, 208
women — **121-124**
words — 30, 84, 86, **94-102,** 110-112, 177, 181, 206-207
work — 123, **142-144,** 152, 163, 220

youth/young — 2, **124-128,** 176-177